Writing about Reading

Shanna Schwartz, Alexandra Marron, and Elizabeth Dunford

Lucy Calkins, series editor

Photography by Peter Cunningham

HEINEMANN ◆ PORTSMOUTH, NH

This book is dedicated to Judah—thanks for being my reading and writing partner. —Shanna

This book is dedicated to Peter, for the thirty years of stories we've shared. —Ali

This book is dedicated to Mom, for every afternoon walk to the library and every book-filled walk home. —Liz

Heinemann
361 Hanover Street
Portsmouth, NH 03801–3912
www.heinemann.com

Offices and agents throughout the world

The authors and publisher wish to thank those who have generously given permission to reprint borrowed material:

Tales for Very Picky Eaters, Theodor Seuss Geisel 2012 Award Statement © American Library Association. Used with permission from the American Library Association. www.ala.org.

Cataloging-in-Publication data is on file with the Library of Congress.

ISBN-13: 978-0-325-04730-0

Production: Elizabeth Valway, David Stirling, and Abigail Heim
Cover and interior designs: Jenny Jensen Greenleaf
Series includes photographs by Peter Cunningham, Nadine Baldasare, and Elizabeth Dunford
Composition: Publishers' Design and Production Services, Inc.
Manufacturing: Steve Bernier

Printed in the United States of America on acid-free paper
20 21 22 23 24 25 PAH 10 9 8 7 6 5
                    April 2020

Acknowledgments

THIS BOOK IS, IN PART, a tribute to two of our favorite authors. Both Kate diCamillo and James Howe hold a special place in our hearts and on our bookshelves. When we think about their contributions to our classrooms and to the childhoods of our students, we are full of gratitude and admiration. Kate has an uncanny ability to write books that are both thoughtful and fun, revealing that which is most idiosyncratic about human nature and giving even the youngest children an opportunity to think deeply and profoundly. We delight every time one of our students calls out, "Wait, those people are teaching their pig like their child. That's crazy!" James also has a respect for young minds. He writes without fear, with an honesty that exudes from every page. James writes in ways that give voice to readers and writers of all ages, giving children the space to figure out what's right and what's wrong, what it means to be yourself, and what it means to find your way in a world that might object to you.

This book stands on many shoulders. First and foremost, we'd like to thank our colleagues at the Teachers College Reading and Writing Project. The work showcased in this book grows out of years' worth of collaboration at the Project. A special thanks to Mary Ehrenworth, whose brilliance guided so much of this unit.

We thank Adele Schroeter, Alison Porcelli, and the second-grade teachers at PS 59, who graciously opened their classrooms to us. The imprints of your teaching are evident throughout this book. We would especially like to thank the second-grade students at PS 59 and the PS 41 Reading and Writing Club, who helped to fill this book with beautiful writing about reading.

Finally, a special thanks to Kate Montgomery, Teva Blair, Abby Heim, and Felicia O'Brien for their precision, patience, and guiding hands. They believed in this book even before it made its way to fruition. For that, we are incredibly grateful.

The class described in this unit is a composite class, with children and partnerships of children gleaned from classrooms in very different contexts, then put together here. We wrote the units this way to bring you both a wide array of wonderful, quirky, various children and also to illustrate for you the predictable (and unpredictable) situations and responses this unit has created in classrooms across the nation and world.

—Shanna, Ali, and Liz

Contents

BEND III Writing Nominations and Awarding Favorite Books

 Registration instructions to access the digital resources that accompany this book may be found on p. viii.

Welcome to the Unit

DURING THIS UNIT OF STUDY, *Writing about Reading,* you will help your children learn to write about beloved books in ways that persuade others to love them as much as they do. You'll help your second-graders form opinions about the books they read, thinking deeply about characters within and across series. In part, then, this is a unit on writing to think—and on doing this complicated grown-up work in ways that are befitting seven-year-olds. Because this is new and ambitious work, the unit will brim with the excitement and energy that comes from that.

The goals of the unit are important ones. You'll help your children learn to state clear opinions and to support these ideas with evidence—work that is at the forefront of the list of expectations for writers as they move on to third grade and beyond.

Most state standards place new demands on second-graders in opinion writing but expect much of the work second-graders do in this genre to be similar to the work they did in first grade, now with increased sophistication. In first grade, your students were expected to "write opinion pieces in which they introduce the topic or name the book they are writing about, state an opinion, supply a reason for the opinion, and provide some sense of closure." Now, in second grade, in addition to introducing the topic they are writing about, your students must also "introduce the book they are writing about" (rather than only name it), "supply reasons that support the opinion," "use linking words (e.g. *because, and, also*) to connect opinion and reasons," and "provide a concluding statement or section." These shifts—introducing the book they are writing, supplying more than one supportive reason, linking parts together, and providing a longer, more formalized ending—are the areas to which you will devote key attention.

If that sounds like heady intellectual work, it is! Bear in mind, though, that in second-graders' writing, this work will sound like this: "In the Frog and Toad story 'Alone,' Toad is more needy than Frog." That is, your children will state opinions and cite evidence from texts they can read and understand, in ways that seven-year-olds can process and deliver.

OVERVIEW OF THE UNIT

Students will begin this unit writing letters—work that will be familiar to those who participated in the kindergarten opinion writing unit on persuasive letters. Across the first bend of this unit, students will draft letters about the characters they've met in their books, formulating opinions and supporting their ideas, providing reasons, and using details and examples from the text to support their claims. Of course, you'll invite students to uncover their opinions about more than just the characters they are getting to know; students will also write about favorite scenes, illustrations across the text, and lessons learned.

Bend I will help students not only to develop opinions about their reading, but to get energy for writing. They will learn to state opinions clearly, retell their stories so that their opinions make sense to readers, and revise their letters before sending them out into the world.

In Bend II, students will focus on raising the level of their letter writing. You'll coach students to engage in some close reading as a way to spark new ideas and to push themselves to deepen their thinking, using their Post-it® notes to elaborate on their opinion pieces. To the untrained eye, there may be portions of this bend where the writing workshop looks strikingly similar to the reading workshop in that students will be learning to read and reread closely to come up with more ideas for opinions, more details and evidence to support their opinions, as well as fun conventions that authors and illustrators use to fancy up and make their writing interesting. Before students send their letters out into the world, they will also participate in a punctuation inquiry and then work to incorporate the conventions that they are noticing in published books into their own writing.

In the final bend, students will shift gears, moving away from persuasive letters into writing that more closely resembles an essay format, as they write to persuade others that their favorite books are worthy of awards. This work will build on the first two bends as students continue to write their opinions about books and support those opinions with reasons and details from the text. However, now they will lift the level of this writing as they learn to incorporate quotations to supply further text evidence, make comparisons between books and across collections of books, as well as add introductions and conclusions, all in the service of teaching and persuading others.

This work leads up to a class book fair, where visitors can be invited to listen to students' book award announcements as a final celebration.

ASSESSMENT

Before you begin this unit of study, you will want to collect some data to support your planning. An on-demand writing assessment, prompting students to construct an opinion piece, will help you assess your students' grasp of this new genre, as well as pinpoint the most current needs of your writers. Your students have grown as writers over the last few months, and you will want to see how the work they have been doing transfers to their work in opinion writing. You may ask students to write an opinion piece, using the prompt from *Writing Pathways: Performance Assessments and Learning Progressions, K–5*:

"Think of a topic or issue that you know and care about, an issue around which you have strong feelings. Tomorrow, you will have forty-five minutes to write an opinion or argument text in which you will write your opinion or claim and tell reasons why you feel that way. When you do this, draw on everything you know about essays, persuasive letters, and reviews. If you want to find and use information from a book or another outside source, you may bring that with you tomorrow. Please keep in mind that you'll have forty-five minutes to complete this, so you will need to plan, draft, revise, and edit in one sitting.

"In your writing, make sure you:

- Name your opinion
- Give reasons and evidence to explain why you have that opinion
- Write an ending"

If you feel that this prompt is not quite right for your second-graders, know that we have had much of this same concern. Ultimately, we decided that to create a true learning progression that reflected pieces at multiple levels that could be compared, we needed to have the same prompt for all students at all grade levels. Of course, you'll probably decide to adapt the prompt to best fit the needs of your particular students. You may decide, for example, to take out the mention of essay writing, as well as to alter the time you grant writers to complete this assessment. If you do adapt this prompt, we highly encourage you to plan how you will do this tailoring in conjunction with your grade team to ensure that you gather consistent data that you can compare across the grade.

Then, you'll likely compare the on-demand writing pieces with the exemplar pieces in the Opinion/Argument Writing Learning Progression (in the *Writing Pathways: Performance Assessments and Learning Progressions, K–5* book) and decide on the approximate level of each writer in your class. You can also determine the next steps you'll take to support each writer.

Your students will now need to create beginnings for their pieces, which do not name their opinion immediately, but rather, introduce readers to the content of their books. They will also need to recognize which reasons are most supportive of their opinion and which are less so. In addition, they will need to create a sense of cohesion within their work. And they will need to start seeing a larger meaning to their pieces to be able to come up with endings that provide more than a sense of closure—ones that are full statements of a conclusion.

During the unit, you should rely on formative assessments, such as student writing, conferring notes from individual conferences, and small-group work, as data-in-hand. Use this information to assess that students are on track and to teach into the things they are not yet grasping to support their progress.

After your students publish their final pieces of opinion writing, you will once again ask them to compose an on-demand piece of writing. This on-demand will serve as a summative assessment, measuring growth across the unit.

GETTING READY

As you prepare for the unit, it is important to gather materials that will support students both as readers and as writers. Because students are writing about reading, it is important that they have high-interest, just-right books at their fingertips throughout the unit. If you have a reading workshop running parallel to the writing workshop, this shouldn't be a problem. If not, you'll want to make sure you fill your classroom with baskets of books that children will be eager to read and write about. Children can write about read-aloud books, old favorites, or books they read last week or last year. It only matters that they have access to these books (to develop new thinking and look for examples to support their ideas) and can read them independently.

You'll find ample paper choices available in the online resources that accompanies this unit. We have found these various kinds of paper particularly successful for each part of the unit (moving children from single sheets of paper to "letter booklets" and finally to nomination paper [denoted with a special award emblem]). The buy-in was spectacular! Of course, you should choose to use whatever paper your children are most comfortable with—paper that will allow them to write with stamina, volume, and organization.

In addition to the texts children write letters and nominations about, you will need to choose two or three texts with which you will model your own writing about reading. These texts will weave through each of the bends and will help you demonstrate each step of the writing process. We chose *Mercy Watson to the Rescue* by Kate DiCamillo and *Pinky and Rex and the Bully* by James Howe. We and the children love these books, not only for their humor, but for their depth and captivating characters. Both texts are replete with places to delve in, read closely, and develop new thinking. Regardless of which texts you choose, be sure your children know them well so they can more closely study the work you do as a *writer*, rather than being distracted by the content of the story or the need to follow an unfolding plot line.

ONLINE DIGITAL RESOURCES

A variety of resources to accompany this and the other Grade 2 Units of Study in Opinion, Information, and Narrative Writing are available in the online resources. To access and download all the digital resources for this grade-level set:

1. Go to **www.heinemann.com** and click the link in the upper right to log in. (If you do not have an account yet, you will need to create one.)

2. **Enter the following registration code** in the box to register your product: **WUOS_GR2**

3. Enter the security information requested, obtained from within your unit book.

4. Once you have registered your product it will appear in the list of "View my registered Online Resources, Videos, and eBooks." (Note: You only need register once; then each time you return to your account, just click the "My Online Resources" link to access these materials.)

(You may keep copies of these resources on up to six of your own computers or devices. By downloading the files you acknowledge that they are for your individual or classroom use and that neither the resources nor the product code will be distributed or shared.)

Writing Letters to Share Ideas about Characters

IN THIS SESSION, you'll teach students that writers are often inspired by their reading and reach out to others to share their ideas about characters.

GETTING READY

✔ A few familiar stories of varying levels, such as *Henry and Mudge, Pinky and Rex, Harry the Dirty Dog* (see Connection)

✔ A touchstone text, to be read to the class beforehand. We chose *Mercy Watson to the Rescue* by Kate DiCamillo (see Teaching)

✔ Chart paper and marker (see Teaching)

✔ Students' books featuring favorite characters. It's quite important that you prompt students, possibly even a day or two before the lesson so they can bring in a book from home if they'd like, to be ready with a book about a favorite character (see Active Engagement).

✔ Writing paper at each table. Most of your writers are probably ready to write on lined paper. You may have paper with various numbers of lines on it to match your writers' handwriting and stamina (see Link).

✔ Envelopes with labels/addresses saying "Readers in Class 202" or whatever your class name is (see Share)

I WILL NEVER FORGET writing my first thank you letter. It was just after my seventh birthday and my mom sat me down at the kitchen table beside a stack of pale purple note cards. "I've made a list of all the presents you got this weekend. Now you should write letters to thank all your friends for coming, and for their lovely gifts."

"All of them?!" I asked in shock and dismay. I glanced at the stack of cards. "But Mom, I had *a bunch* of friends at my birthday party!"

"And they all brought you lovely presents," she retorted. "Oh, and we can't forget Grandma and Grandpa or your cousins either!" I begrudgingly wrote over fifteen thank you notes that day, wishing I could just send the presents back and call it a day. *If it takes this much work, I don't really want that sweater*, I thought. Letters belonged to a class of decorum I'd yet to understand.

As the years passed, though, letter writing took on its own form and function in my life. I continued to write thank you notes for presents I received, gradually with more grace than I had when I was seven, and I found other purposes for the genre, as well. I'd write to keep in touch with camp friends or classmates who had moved away. We'd pour our hearts onto paper, swearing we couldn't last another day without seeing each other. I wrote to express anger (mean, scathing letters slipped into a locker), to apologize (detailed, excusing letters slipped under a bedroom door), and to vent (in a secret notebook passed between high school friends). Perhaps most importantly, I learned that writing letters was a valuable form of persuasion when one sought desperately to stay another week at sleep-away camp, to beg forgiveness after an incident of teenage angst, or to get that coveted job.

Some say that email has led to the death of the letter, and they aren't completely wrong. It is rare that we receive a letter in our mailboxes these days. But the spirit, purpose, and form of persuasive letter writing is ever-present: in email exchanges, online blogs, applications, and editorials. Letter writing, in its simplest form, is about expressing an idea or sentiment and appealing to an audience. If your writers have grown up working within *Units of Study for Teaching Writing*, they will understand this. They will have written letters suggesting ideas for solving problems seen in their classroom and given their opinions about their "best in show" selections, backing up those opinions with reasons and some details.

"In this unit, we move into a specific form of opinion letters—writing opinions about books and using evidence from the text to support those ideas."

In this unit, we move into a specific form of opinion letters—writing opinions about books and using evidence from the text to support those ideas. This work should build on the opinion writing children have done previously. You'll want to remind them that the strategies they used to argue persuasively for a cleaner classroom are the same skills and strategies they'll use to argue in support of an idea about a book.

In this session, you start children off on their letter-writing adventures by teaching them to write passionately about characters they love. You know that feeling: when you've read a book and you love a character so much that you can hardly bear to finish the story. One of the only comforts as you put the book reluctantly down is to persuade your friends to read the same story, and then it's like your time with the character isn't really over, because you'll keep talking and writing about it. Francis Spufford, author of *The Child That Books Built*, writes about how when he was a child he kept reading the Narnia series over and over again because he couldn't bear to be parted from Edmund, Lucy, and Mr. Tumnus the faun. Later, he found himself writing about Narnia and his childhood days spent with those fictional friends. Writing about books keeps characters alive for us.

In this first bend of the unit, you'll teach children what's often worth including when writing letters about books and offer strategies for how to write even better letters. As you set off on this unit, expect that not every letter will include clearly stated opinions or supporting reasons and details. That's okay. This is a journey, and you are, in fact, reinforcing the idea that thinking can be a journey that is supported through writing.

Writing Letters to Share Ideas about Characters

CONNECTION

Inspire your children with energy around letters about books, by first recalling their experience with letters and then describing how letters about books bring together two things they love—writing and books.

"Writers, come to the meeting area, and as you come, bring that book we spoke about—one about a favorite character." I motioned to the children to gather their materials and come together as I reminded them. The children began to gather, holding copies of *Magic Treehouse*, *Frog and Toad*, *Spiderman*, and other personal favorites.

I waited a moment for the children to gather.

"Come close, children, with your books. I'm really eager to introduce to you some new work that I just know you are ready for and will love. It's not *totally* new work, because it's letter writing, and I know you've written letters before. And it's writing about books, and I know you've done *that* before as well."

"Writers, let's begin by remembering the kinds of letters you've probably written. As I say a few kinds, nod if you've written one of these kinds of letters." I looked around at the children and began to describe familiar letters. "Nod if you've written persuasive letters, thank you letters, notes to say you're sorry, letters to grandparents, letters to your teacher, letters to friends, letters to the principal!"

As I listed various kinds of letters, many of the children nodded.

"Well, there's one kind of letter that will be an absolute favorite. It's letters about books. I love letters, and I love books, so I bet you're not surprised that this is one of my favorite kinds of writing."

Have at hand a few familiar books with strong characters to visually call to mind some of these beloved characters.

I looked at the children as if I were letting them in on a secret. As I spoke, I flourished a few books with favorite characters (*Henry and Mudge*, *Ruby the Copycat*, *Pinky and Rex*). "Here's why letters about books are so great. You know that feeling, when you read a book with characters you love, and you're sad when the story ends?"

Just the simple invitation to come to the meeting area, carrying with you a book about the character you love most in all of literature—what an invitation! Consider if you received such a request. Wouldn't the sheer process of reviewing and selecting be a wonderful one? And imagine sitting in a circle, with all your classmates, and seeing that each has brought a book containing his or her favorite character to the meeting area.

These comments reflect the kindergarten letter-writing work and the first-grade reviews that we assume many of your children experienced if your school has adopted Units of Study for Teaching Writing. *Otherwise, you could instead say something like "I'm pretty sure you've written letters, and I know you've had a lot of smart conversations about books."*

It's helpful at the beginning of a unit of study to recall for children that they already know something about the kind of writing you are embarking on. Often at the start of a unit, or the beginning of a new bend in these units, you'll notice opportunities to remind students that they are not empty vessels, that they need to transfer and apply skills they carry forward from prior teaching and learning.

The children nodded, possibly remembering their experience with independent reading, read-aloud, or lap reading.

"I see you nodding. It's as if the characters become our friends, and we want to keep them! We don't want to *give up* Pinky and Rex, or Henry and Mudge, or Ruby the Copycat! And you know what, writers? When you write about books, it's as if you get to keep the characters. You keep thinking about them, and you share your ideas with your friends, and then you never have to feel as if these characters are gone.'"

❖ **Name the teaching point.**

"Today, I want to teach you that writers who love stories (which is most writers!) often write letters to each other about favorite characters. One thing writers often do in these letters is explain their opinions about these characters."

I said "gone" as if it were a tragedy, and grimaced, clinging to the books I had flourished before.

TEACHING

Demonstrate one way to get started writing a letter, by recalling opinions you have about a character.

"Well, writers, I asked you to bring a book to the meeting area today that has a character you really love, and I did the same. I brought *Mercy Watson*. I have *a lot* of opinions about Mercy."

I flipped through a few pages of *Mercy Watson to the Rescue*, murmuring opinions aloud about the story. "I *love* how she eats buttered toast! I think it's *hilarious* when Mercy runs around the yard with Eugenia chasing her! Mercy is such a *silly* pig!"

The children laughed. "Okay, writers, there are tons of things we could write about Mercy. So why don't you help me start a letter to class 202."

Demonstrate how you might begin a letter, recalling what students already learned about opinion writing from prior units of study.

I moved to the chart paper and quickly jotted as I thought aloud. "Let me think. We should probably start with some sort of introduction, like you learned to do in first grade when writing persuasive book reviews. This way our reader will know that we are talking about a character in a book. So maybe this letter can start":

Sometimes you can raise the level of students' initial thinking and writing just by letting them hear the kind of language you are hoping for—in this case, what opinions about characters sound like. Your children are probably very familiar with expressing and backing up ideas about characters from reading workshop, but it still helps them transfer these skills to writing when you model this language. Also, acting as if coming up with ideas is "no big deal" will set a positive tone for this new writing work.

You'll notice that I am embedding a little tucked tip here, asking children to recall what they learned about introductions in prior years and apply it to this new situation. I will teach the components of a strong letter later, more explicitly, but many children will benefit from even just this little reminder.

> Dear Readers in Class 202,
>
> Do you love reading books with funny characters? Well then, you'll love to read about Mercy Watson. She is HILARIOUS! She's a pig who lives in a house!

Prompt students to explain ideas, and have them join you as you think of some examples to support the idea you've grown about your character.

I looked up for a moment. "Writers, we know it's always important to explain ourselves, to give examples. So right now, it's our job to explain, to say more about how Mercy is hilarious. I bet you're thinking some of the same things I am. Give a thumbs up if you can think of something funny about Mercy!"

Thumbs went up in the air. "Let's add some more to this letter. As I do so, turn and whisper to your partner anything you think we should add about Mercy being funny." As the children whispered, I quickly added:

> Dear Readers in Class 202,
>
> Do you love reading books with funny characters? Well then, you'll love to read about Mercy Watson. She is HILARIOUS! She's a pig who lives in a house! She gets to eat buttered toast too. Mercy even has her own bed, in her own room—in her own house!

Debrief your steps.

I turned back to the children. "Well class, Mercy really is hilarious. That's why they call her the porcine wonder! Do you see what I did as a letter writer? I flipped through my book for a moment and reminded myself of some of my opinions. You may not even need to do that; you may already have opinions! Then I started off my letter by introducing my reader to the book and character. Then, I said my opinion (that Mercy Watson is hilarious). But I didn't stop there! Next, I explained myself by giving a bunch of examples of how Mercy is so funny."

ACTIVE ENGAGEMENT

Invite your students to share their opinions about characters in their own books as a way to plan their writing.

"Writers, I know that each of you brought a favorite book or two to the meeting area. Let's take a moment now to plan *your* writing. What opinions do you have about your characters? What examples can you think of? When you have some opinions about your character, put a thumb in the air. I know you'll have a lot to say, because you've chosen characters you love."

I waited about a minute until many thumbs were up. Then I said, "Turn and tell your partner your opinions about a character in your book."

I listened in as Petra talked to her partner. She opened up *Magic Tree House* and began, "I get so annoyed with Jack! Jack should listen to Annie more."

Again, you'll notice that I channel students to participate without actually asking for their input. In this way, I am assured that they are all thinking alongside me, engaged in the work at hand, but I avoid derailing the minilesson (or the focus of my modeling) with student responses that may or may not be on point.

We've chosen to start the children off with examples, and move later in the unit to the more abstract thinking of "reasons and examples." In reaching for both, you'll be teaching world-class standard expectations for third grade. Our classroom research has found that developmentally, children often come up with examples first, as they recall concrete details from texts.

There are many options for the active engagement, and you will see different variations across this unit. I could have had children continue on with our Mercy Watson letter, asking them to develop a second idea about Mercy and some examples to go with it. Instead, I chose to use the active engagement to help children transfer this work to their own book mostly because I know that transference can be one of the hardest parts of learning! This affords us the opportunity to coach the students as they try this work independently.

Her partner, Levi, shook his head, "Well, but Jack is the smart one. He's smart, like when he reads about the lions or the polar bears—then he knows important stuff."

Seizing this teaching opportunity, I called the children back together. "Writers, Petra and Levi are both reading a book in the *Magic Tree House* series. Petra shared with Levi that she feels annoyed with Jack, because he is always giving Annie a hard time. Levi disagreed. He feels that Jack is more important because he is smart. Wouldn't you love for them to write you letters, trying to convince you to like Annie or Jack better?

"Here's the important thing to remember, though." I leaned in close and made sure all eyes were on me. "Petra and Levi didn't just say, 'I think Annie is brave. I think Jack is smart.' They *described* more about their opinion by giving examples from the text. For instance, Levi said that Jack is smart because he is always reading and he writes everything down."

LINK

Invite your writers to go to it as letter writers. Remind them where to find paper. Most importantly, reinforce that they have a lot to write about.

"Writers, let's spend today writing letters to each other—to the readers in our class, class 202. After all, we're all reading and writing buddies and we'll want to know each other's opinions. And you have so many opinions about your characters. Those conversations you just had are really your writing plans, and you're clearly going to have a lot to write about in your letter. Remember that whenever you write a letter about a book, you can introduce your ideas to your reader and then give some examples to explain yourself."

I made a "get-to-it" motion with my hands, toward the tables and paper. "Let's get to it, while our ideas are fresh in our heads."

Listen to your children during this active engagement, and you may see quick tips that you can extend to other writers. For instance, these children were both reading the same book, so as one writer gave an opinion, their conversation led to a few other opinions. You might seize this opportunity to reinforce the value of letter writing (as a form of persuasion) and the need for evidence to back up an idea. You might gather children who are reading the same books, and nudge them to have similar kinds of conversations.

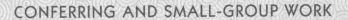

Spreading Writing Energy

THE REAL WORK OF THIS FIRST DAY will be for you to encourage and excite and raise the energy of everyone in the room as you spread little bits of advice, usually through sharing student writing. You can do this in a number of ways. First and foremost, you will likely want to move around the room oohing and ahhing and laughing, and saying aloud little bits of what children are writing. You may comment about how much you like the books the children have chosen or how the letters already have you wanting to read books you don't know. In other words, spread joy and excitement around the room. When the children feel your enthusiasm, they will grow that same feeling themselves.

Another way to increase energy and spread advice is to do quick table compliment conferences. You can try this by simply finding a child who has done something worth mentioning. Maybe one student wrote her opinion about a character and then gave lots of information from the book to support that one opinion. Or perhaps, another child wrote about more than one character in a story, like Henry *and* Mudge.

In other words, you can choose any child who has done something that other children can try. You might sit down next to this writer and then call for the attention of all the children at the table, saying something like, "Red table, can I have your eyes please? I want to tell you a bit about what Eliza just did. She wrote her opinion about her character and then she gave the reader a whole bunch of examples from the book to prove her idea. "Writers, this will help Eliza's reader really believe her opinion! Put a thumb up if you think you will try giving more information from the book as examples." You may decide to conduct a number of these table compliment conferences around the room, thus sharing little bits of successful writing and giving other children small, manageable ideas for how to keep writing.

As you move around the room complimenting and teaching, remember to take note of what children are doing from the start. If your students are all writing opinions and

MID-WORKSHOP TEACHING   The Structure of a Letter

"Writers, can I have your attention please?" I stood next to Sebastian. "Sebastian just reminded me that some of you might like a reminder about the parts of a letter. Sebastian has written, 'Dear Reader.' That's such a good greeting, or opening! If you didn't write a greeting at the top of your letter, go ahead and add that now—and make sure to capitalize the first letter of *Dear* and *Reader* and put a comma afterward." I waited a moment. "Would you and your partner look over each others' work? Is there a greeting, and is it capitalized and punctuated correctly?"

Then I said, "Writers, this is so great. When you write letters, it is so helpful to put a greeting at the beginning to tell the reader who the letter is for. Oh, and you'll probably remember from writing letters that you have a closing at the end to let them know who the letter is from." I pointed to our class letter and said, "I'm going to add 'Sincerely yours, comma, Class 202.' I quickly jotted that closing. "Did you notice the way I capitalized that? You might want to write that closing too, or you could just write, 'From, comma, Emma.' Choose what works best for you, and make sure to capitalize and punctuate the opening and closing correctly."

giving reasons from the get go, you may need to think about how that will affect the way you teach the Session 2 share, in which the teaching point encourages children to add reasons. If your children are writing about a main character, you may encourage some children to think about other characters to help them write with greater depth. This is a great day to be on the lookout for trends that can inform upcoming teaching.

Getting Letters to Readers

Ask your readers to prepare their letters by putting them in envelopes.

"Writers, bring your letters to the meeting area, please." I waited until the children were gathered. In front of me I had stacks of envelopes. I had already labeled each envelope "Readers in Class 202."

"Writers, whenever you write a letter, you need to make sure that readers get to read them. Today we wrote letters for readers in this classroom. So let's put our letters in envelopes, and how about if we tuck these envelopes inside the books where the characters live? That way, readers can read our letters when they choose these books. If you wrote a letter about a book you brought from home, I have a basket here marked 'Family Favorites.' Go ahead, take an envelope for your letter. If you wrote two letters, take two!"

Once the children had envelopes, I said, "Writers, let's all get our letters delivered. Find the book basket where your book lives and put this envelope right inside so readers can find it. I bet later in reading workshop, you'll be pleased if there's a letter tucked inside a book when you are book shopping!"

A minute later I asked the children to put their eyes on me and said dramatically, "Writers, congratulations! You have just published letters about books!"

You could, of course, invite your children to address the envelopes themselves. Certainly they'll want to begin to address their own envelopes as they decide on specific readers across the week, and usually you want children to do everything for themselves as writers. Because the launch of the unit already poses some logistical challenges, and to use every possible moment for writing, we decided to have some envelopes prepared in advance.

Getting Energy for Writing by Talking

IN THIS SESSION, you'll teach students that writers use conversations as rehearsals for writing, and they need to be mindful of their writing energy.

GETTING READY

✔ A student to model with for the demonstration, prepped beforehand (see Teaching)

✔ *Mercy Watson to the Rescue* or another touchstone text (see Teaching)

✔ Class shared writing, started in Session 1 (see Share)

PICTURE TIMES WHEN YOU'VE TALKED ABOUT BOOKS: you're in a book club or you see a friend reading a juicy book you've already read. You and your reading buddy practically fall over each other recalling favorite parts. "I loved the part when . . . ," you'll say. "Could you believe . . . ?" your buddy will query. "Oh, wait, what about *that* part," you'll continue. You'll go on and on about parts that were wonderful or dreadful or shocking until you begin to run dry. Then your energy for ideas flags. If you're in a book club, your club will turn to the snacks and beverages and chitchat, which makes book clubs such great social groups as well as reading groups.

If you were writing buddies as well as reading buddies, though, you would have your notebooks open, or your iPads fired up as you talked. You would probably eschew the postconversation snacks in favor of turning on your laptop. "Listen," you'd say, "I think I'm ready to do some writing. Let's talk again later." The Reading and Writing Project consists of reading and writing buddies, and the art of talking as rehearsal for writing has been fine-tuned. Everyone is inducted into the understanding that it's no insult to say, "Okay, that's enough talk. I need to go write," and everyone learns to ask, "Do you need to talk more, or do you have enough to start writing?" Getting a colleague off the phone is as easy as getting a colleague on the phone—a *crucial* writing skill. Buddies support one another as writers.

Often writers find that talking is the first step. That's the "on the phone" part of rehearsal. If you're engaged in this unit of study, that means your children are reading and talking about books, and they're probably talking about their books across the day, inside and outside of the workshop. Your children probably have conversations about your class read-aloud books. They surely have conversations with their reading partners. They may have small-group book talks and conversations in the library as they search for new reads. These reading conversations have great potential as rehearsals for writing. The trick, though, is to fulfill that potential. You want to get them off the phone! How often have you heard teachers lament, "He says so much more than he writes," or "If only she would write a quarter of what she says"?

In this session, you'll teach your students that their conversations about their books can be very important to them as writers, *and* you'll teach them to begin to be mindful of when they should go from talking to writing. As soon as they have started on some strong opinions, ones they're excited about, they should start writing while their energy is high.

"If you're engaged in this unit of study, that means your children are reading and talking about books, and they're probably talking about their books across the day, inside and outside of the workshop."

This is a session where you can tuck in some writing tips to reinforce work that some students will do naturally. For instance, while the session is explicitly about maximizing partners' writing energy, you can also tuck in another collecting strategy—writing about favorite parts of a story. And you can work toward making smart writing choices and using time wisely. While it's only the second day of the unit, by the end of your lesson students should be able to make significant writing choices. They might combine writing about characters and favorite parts. They might write different letters about the same book or new letters about new books. They should definitely decide when to stop talking and start writing, which means you'll have to let them monitor their conversations rather than simply dictate when time is up.

By this time in the year, it's important to hold students to all the strong writing habits they've grown, especially that of making smart decisions as writers when they think they're "done."

Getting Energy for Writing by Talking

CONNECTION

Recount for your students the conversations you've heard them have across the day about books.

"Yesterday, all day long, I was alert to whenever you were talking about books. I think because you're writing these letters, my ears perked up whenever I heard a book conversation. And you know what? I heard you talk about books all across the day! I heard you during reading workshop, of course, when you talked to your reading partners. And I heard you when you were unpacking your backpacks and some of you were telling each other about the books you were reading. And I heard you during book shopping, when some of you were recommending books to each other. I even heard you talking about new ideas you were learning from the books you are reading in science.

"Writers, all that conversation is a great way to practice for your letters. After all, you're talking about your books, and in your letters, you're writing about your books. So you should be chock-full of ideas."

Give your students some feedback on how often they talk but then don't really get to write. Then invite them to think about how to get better at getting to writing.

"Here's one thing I noticed, though, writers. When you talk about your books, you talk and talk, until you don't have any more to say. And then you know what usually happens? You stop talking and go back to reading or to unpacking your backpack or to book shopping. This is not necessarily a bad thing, but because we want our talking to lead to *more writing*, I think we need to ask ourselves, 'What would it look like if your book *conversations* became *rehearsals* for writing? What would have to happen as you finished your conversation?

"Are you asking yourself that question writers?" I paused for a moment for students to think but didn't call on them, letting the question sit in the air. Then I said, "I've been thinking about this, and I think we need to make sure you have as much energy for writing about your books as you do for talking about them!"

 **Name the teaching point.**

"Writers, today I want to teach you that writers often rehearse for their writing with a partner by talking through the big ideas they are having about their books. To maximize their energy for writing, they talk about big ideas and often

◆ COACHING

In today's connection, we hope to help children see that what they are learning in writing workshop stands on the shoulders of work they've done before. Books are an integral part of our classroom community, so we hope to help children make connections across the curriculum and see the ways texts (and talking about texts) inform all areas of learning.

You'll notice that we've tried to make today's teaching feel incredibly responsive. This is a great way to garner engagement and personal investment in your children. Children, and all people really, want to be acknowledged. By saying "I've been watching you. I've noticed a few things. Today's teaching is especially designed for you," we help each child feel seen and heard in the classroom.

save the smaller details for their writing. That means as soon as they have some big ideas and are energized to write, they stop talking and get right to writing!"

TEACHING

Let your writers know that you want to help them get better at truly rehearsing for writing. Alert them to the trickiness of maximizing their energy for writing.

"Writers, let's give this a try, and as we do, let's also think about other ideas we can write about in our letters. Yesterday you learned that writing about characters is a good generating strategy. Another good strategy is writing about favorite parts. After all, you talk about those all the time, right?"

I waited while the children nodded in agreement. Then I continued. "Writers, I'm not worried about you finding favorite parts of your books. I know from listening to you talk about books that you can do that. What I'd like to help you get better at today is making sure that your partner conversation really maximizes your energy for writing."

Give an "antidemonstration," in which you show what it looks like to lose energy by continuing to talk even after you come up with an idea for writing.

"This work is a little trickier than you think. Here's what might happen if we're not careful, writers." I started the next bit with an energetic tone, which gradually became slower and less energetic. "Sometimes, what happens is that you talk about your big ideas, and you seem excited to write about them. Then you go on talking. You might talk about smaller ideas. Maybe you talk about lots and lots and lots of details. And then," I made my voice slow down, and my body slump over, "you have no energy left for writing."

The children giggled. I perked up again. "So here's my tip: the trick is, talk to your partner just until you have some big ideas for writing. Then stop! Save the details for your writing. That way you'll be excited to go write. Your partner can help you get lots of energy for writing."

Do a quick demonstration, or "fishbowl," of talking through an idea with a partner, and then of being mindful of stopping while you have energy to write, using a student with whom you've rehearsed.

"I'm going to rehearse my writing with Sam. Watch for how I talk with my partner about favorite parts. And watch for how Sam helps me maximize my energy for writing. Okay, here goes!

"Sam, I'm thinking of writing about my favorite parts of *Mercy Watson to the Rescue*." I picked up the book and used an energetic tone. "Well, one of my *most* favorite parts of Mercy Watson is when the bed falls through the ceiling."

Sam nodded enthusiastically. I went on, my voice still energetic. "I love the part about the bed falling because really, it's Mercy's fault that the bed falls, because she snuck onto it in the middle of the night. And I *love* how it starts to fall all the way through the ceiling and then the Watsons are stuck. That really made me laugh." I let my voice begin to flag

We expect that children already know how to identify their favorite part of a book and therefore take this opportunity to remind them of this prior knowledge before quickly moving onto something new. We often refer to this as "tucked teaching"—little tips we tuck in as we teach larger strategies.

If you've done fishbowl demonstrations in your classroom before, students will be used to watching this kind of role playing/enactment. For this fishbowl, you are demonstrating work that is actually beyond students' current skill level rather than calling on something a partnership has already demonstrated, so you'll want to rehearse beforehand, and it will really be more role playing than authentic partner talk. If you have two strong students who can carry off this fishbowl demonstration, you could gather the class to study them.

and drag. "Hmm, I guess another favorite part might be . . . maybe when . . . well . . . I liked the Watsons' faces when the bed begins to fall, and I like her bed too . . . It's neat she has a bed . . . though sometimes she naps on a couch too. In the living room. . . . "

As we had planned, Sam interrupted me. "Wait a second, it seems like you were ready to write. You know, like, about the part you love where the bed fell through the ceiling. You seem really excited about that idea. Write it down while you're excited! Go start your letter! I can't wait to read your letter later!"

The children giggled at how much Sam sounded like the teacher.

Recap what happened in your fishbowl demonstration, emphasizing how writers often talk past big ideas, and partners can help each other stop talking and start writing.

"Writers, do you see how when I talked with Sam, I started out with a lot of energy, but then as I kept talking, I began to run out, especially when I began to go on and on about tiny details? And did you see how Sam helped me stay really excited to write? 'Don't tell me more,' he said, 'write it down while you're excited!' That really made me want to go write—right away!"

ACTIVE ENGAGEMENT

Give students an opportunity to rehearse for writing by talking in partnerships. Remind them to stop each other when it sounds like they have built up their writing energy.

"Let's give this a try right now, writers. Partners, quickly decide which one of you has some ideas about your book. Maybe you have some favorite parts you're excited to talk about. If both of you have ideas, just practice now with one of you. Okay, Partner 1, you be the writer who is talking about favorite parts. Partner 2, you listen carefully. When it seems like your partner is excited about his or her ideas, stop him or her! You might say 'Wait, it sounds like you're ready to write your letter! Get your pencil, quickly!'

"Turn and talk, writers, and be mindful of that energy to write. You need every bit!"

As the children talked, I circulated, whispering in to the listener, saying prompts such as "Oh, that writer does seem excited. Listen. Think about getting the most out of that writing energy!"

After a minute or two, I called the children back.

"Writers," I said. "I like how some of you stopped your partner. 'You should go start your letter,' I heard. And 'Wait, don't tell me more, write it down!' I also heard some of you stopping yourself, saying 'Wait, I need to go write now.'"

You can really use your body language and tone of voice to play up this drama, so that you go from energetic to clearly flagging. If you've rehearsed with this student, he or she should now interrupt you. Your partner could even sound just a little bit bossy here.

Notice that I only talk to the listening partner. This helps the children keep their focus on the partnership work, rather than shifting their focus to me.

LINK

Send students off, reminding them of the various options they have for independent work time.

"Writers, from now on, when you are rehearsing your ideas with a partner, be mindful of your writing energy and make sure you maximize it.

"Right now, you have a few choices." As I listed the next three choices I counted off on my fingers as I named each idea, to make it clear I was naming three. "One: you might want to start a letter about what you just rehearsed, about favorite parts of your books. Two: you might want to add onto a letter you started yesterday. After all, you can write about characters *and* favorite parts in one letter. Three: a few of you want to continue your conversation for a moment, so that both partners get to rehearse. Quickly, make a decision about what's best for you as a writer today."

After a moment, I continued on. "Off you go, writers. Spin all that energy into writing! Yesterday, you tucked your letters into books all around our classroom library, so they'll find their way into the hands of readers. But let's plan, for the rest of this week, to keep your pieces in your folders. That way, you'll have opportunities to write and revise your letters, making them the best they can be, before sending them to your readers."

I give the children an opportunity to make their own decision here. One way to develop independence in your writers is to assist them in making their own decisions.

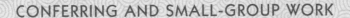

Turning to Familiar Strategies When Writing in a New Genre

DEVELOPING WRITING ENERGY IS AN IMPORTANT JOB at the beginning of a unit. Likely, you spent much of yesterday's conferring time working to spread writing energy around the classroom, and today your minilesson focused on developing writing energy as well. For many children, this extra enthusiasm from you, and now from their partner work, will do the trick. Your enthusiasm will help most children find their own excitement for this new work. But there may still be a child or two who is off to a tough start. Finding internal motivation for writing can be difficult, but it is always worth it. So when you see the child who sits down, writes "Dear Reader," and then freezes, you will feel the pull of gravity toward that writer. Whenever we start new genres, a few students feel as if the whole world is being reinvented. For these writers, simple reassurance and a reminder that they still know stuff even though the genre is new, may get them past that initial stage when they look at you like a deer caught in headlights. The trick is to make sure that you are not doing all of the work for them.

You might begin with these frozen writers by having them tell you how they've gotten started in the past. Perhaps they simply need to remind themselves that they can still sketch before writing. Sketching the character or a favorite part and then writing about that moment in a letter may help a lot of your writers and is something even some adult writers do. Or maybe they often rehearse their writing by planning its parts across their fingers. As you approach your children who seem stuck, think about what you know they know.

"I'm stuck. I don't know what else to write," said Zac as I approached him. I looked down at Zac's paper, and sure enough, it was full of white space. He had chosen paper with close to twenty lines, and he had filled only three. It read:

Dear Reader,

I can't stop reading My Weird School.
The principal is so funny.

MID-WORKSHOP TEACHING **Using Your Partner when Your Writing Slows Down, without Slowing Down Your Partner**

"Writers, could I have your eyes on me for a moment? Rimari just did something really great that we should share with our writing buddies.

"Rimari realized that he was slowing down as a writer. He wrote a lot about one favorite part of his story, the part he'd told his partner about. But then when he went to write about another favorite part, he wasn't sure what to say. So this is what Rimari said to his partner. He said, 'Hey, Dante, can I talk about another favorite part with you? I think it would help me. But if you want to wait, that's okay. I don't want to use up all *your* energy.'"

I looked around at the children. "Writers, there are two great things that Rimari did. One is that he realized he could turn to his partner for help when his writing slowed down. You might do that too. You might ask your partner for help, and talk through another idea when you feel your energy drop. And the second thing he did was, he asked *when* his partner could talk, so he didn't interrupt his partner's writing. Isn't that great? It's so important to be able to talk and also to decide *when* to talk.

"Writers, I'll leave it to you when you might want to talk with your partner to get more energy for writing. And I'll be ready to admire you for being thoughtful about *when* to talk, so that your partner's energy for writing stays strong."

I knew how this was going to go. Zac liked to call me over for help before trying much on his own. In this conference, I knew right away that I was going to use a very light touch. I was going to get Zac to realize that he already knew how to get started. Since the minilesson was about partnership rehearsal, I thought I would try the proficient partner approach to this conference. By playing the role of Zac's partner I could gently nudge him, without jumping into the rescue. "Zac, I'll be your partner for a moment, rather than your teacher. If I were your partner, and I couldn't figure out how to keep going, what might you tell me? I just can't seem to figure out what to write."

Zac looked at me in bemusement for a moment. I helped a little more. "Oh, partner Zac," I hammed it up, "I'm stuck as a writer. You know what? I don't even want to write. I'd rather draw something."

Zac's eyes lit up. "You could do that! You could draw something. When you're really stuck, that helps a lot!"

"*Oh*, I can draw? Do you draw to help yourself get started sometimes?" I asked this question with a wink, knowing that drawing often helps Zac. He nodded and smiled too. He got the joke. "Anything else I can do?"

Zac understood that I was coaching him to coach himself now. "Yeah, after I draw the picture I can use all the details in my picture to help me write more." He paused, thinking for a moment. "I'm going to draw the part of *My Weird School* when the principal kisses the pig. It is so funny. And then I can write all about it!"

I was tempted to just leave at this point, since Zac was already sketching on the back of his paper. But I wanted to make sure Zac recognized that he had just gotten *himself* "unstuck," and I wanted him to put some words around that so that he could do it again next time, without me. "Zac, can you just say what you did to get yourself going?"

Zac looked up, a little surprised I was still there. "Yeah, I'm drawing, and then I'm going to write."

"So, next time you are stuck, do you think this strategy can help you?" I knew Zac would not only have more to his letter soon, but he might even feel less stuck next time he started a new kind of writing. Later, I looked over his shoulder, and Zac had written on about men kissing pigs (see Figure 2–1).

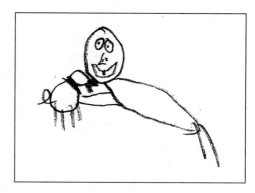

FIG. 2–1   Zac's quick sketch helps him get "unstuck" as a writer.

FIG. 2–2   Zac's letter fills a page after his sketch gets him started.

Dear Reader,

I can't stop reading My Weird School. The principal is so funny. Once I read it and I wondered, "Why did the principal kiss a pig on the lips?" I wonder because it's not average for a grown man to kiss a pig. It's also weird because in my school the principals help people out with their problems. It's also weird that the teacher is from another planet called Etinarg.

Sincerely, Zac

Explaining Reasons to Your Partner and Your Reader

Gather children and invite them to share reasons for their opinions about characters, highlighting the word *because* as a linking word.

Once students had settled in with their materials, I began.

"Writers, today you got a lot of writing done, because you rehearsed so well with a partner and started writing while your energy was strong. Well done! I want to give you a tip that's especially important for opinion writers. When writers give an opinion, like an opinion about a character, or a favorite part, they also give reasons. And to get to reasons, the word *because* is really helpful. Listen for a moment as I read you some opinions that also have a *because* part that explains the opinion."

I read aloud some opinion statements from the class shared writing as well as those that I had gathered from students.

> Mercy Watson is unusual BECAUSE she lives in a house. In the house she has her own bed, and she naps on a couch, and she gets to eat buttered toast.
>
> The little girl in Owl Moon is a good kid BECAUSE she always does what her Pa tells her. Like when she doesn't make noise because her Pa told her to be quiet when you go looking at owls.
>
> Pinky is a bad brother BECAUSE he's mean to Amanda. He won't play with her, and he is sort of mean when he speaks to her.

"Writers, when you rehearse with a partner, asking your partner to explain reasons is really helpful. So if your partner says that Annie is really brave, then there should be a *because*.

"Let's try this. Think of one of your opinions about your book. When you have an opinion, try telling your partner the opinion and reasons. Partners, listen for *because*."

The children turned and talked. After a few minutes, I gathered them back.

"Writers, whenever you rehearse or write opinions, remember to back up your opinions with reasons. Using the word *because* really helps get you to your reasons."

Calling up each child to read her own writing during a share session can sometimes dilute the energy from the real purpose of your share. Here I read little bits from students' work in order to keep the focus on the teaching point.

Writers Generate More Letters

Developing New Opinions by Looking at Pictures

A NY TEACHER OR LOVER OF CHILDREN'S BOOKS respects the power of the illustrations that accompany the text. They set a tone for the book, immediately sweeping the reader into the comical world of Mercy Watson, the realistic and turbulent world of Pinky and Rex, or the complex, somewhat symbolic world of Frog and Toad. As adults, we understand the genius behind the work of illustrators. Is it any coincidence that Frog is depicted as taller and older looking than Toad, appearing to be more of a father than a friend? How about the picture of Mercy Watson with a golden halo around her, lit up like an angel? Or even the picture of the bed falling through the ceiling, viewed from below, with Mrs. Watson's plump form causing it to sink even further.

The artist of the Mercy Watson series, Chris Van Dusen, was clearly having a ball when drawing these illustrations. Like many illustrators of children's books, Van Dusen doesn't illustrate the scenes that are already depicted in detail through the words. Instead, he layers the text with additional meaning and nuances by adding extra details to his illustrations. In fact, the pictures offer a lot of secrets to readers who pay attention. It's no accident that most state standards invite young readers to compare information gleaned from illustrations to information gained from printed text. Most children's books set readers up to do this kind of work.

Paying attention to the pictures should be one more way that writers find things to say about their books. What you'll probably find is that the more children notice, the more they have to say and the more they have to write. As they write more, they'll become closer readers and stronger writers and so on. You're hopefully lucky enough to be teaching writing workshop and reading workshop, where these parallels are so beautiful. Your children will be better writers because they read, and better readers because they write.

IN THIS SESSION, you'll teach students that writers look closely at the pictures in their books to help them develop opinions.

GETTING READY

✔ *Mercy Watson to the Rescue* or other touchstone text (see Connection and Teaching)

✔ Chart paper and marker (see Link)

✔ A basket of favorite class texts or the books that students have chosen to write about (see Active Engagement)

✔ "Uncovering Our Opinions about Books" chart (see Link and Share)

✔ Opinion Writing Checklist, Grades 2 and 3 (see Conferring and Small-Group Work)

✔ A piece of student writing that includes the use of parts of a book to get ideas for writing (see Share)

Writers Generate More Letters

Developing New Opinions by Looking at Pictures

CONNECTION

Gather children and recall an image from your shared story. Choose a scene that is portrayed in a picture rather than in the words of the text.

"Writers, I woke up last night, because there was a noise in my house. I lay there for a moment, wondering and listening. And as I lay there, I tried to think of other things than the noise. Have you ever done that? Tried *not* to think of noises in the dark?"

There were nods from children at the thought of noises in the dark.

"Hmm, I see you nodding. Well, I thought of the pig we know, who also lay in the dark—and then how Mrs. Watson let her get into bed with her and Mr. Watson. I was thinking how *I* wouldn't let a pig get in bed with me!"

I picked up the book, opening the pages and flipping through them. "Writers, this morning I tried and tried to find the part where it says that Mrs. Watson let Mercy into bed, but it doesn't say it anywhere! Then I began to wonder if I had gotten it wrong."

Go back to the text to show that the scene you recall wasn't created through the printed words.

I showed the children the pages and read aloud some of the words as I did. As I did so, some of them began to whisper and nudge, saying, "It's in the picture!"

"Writers, I can see you're having the same realization I did! That the part that I love, about Mrs. Watson letting Mercy into bed, wasn't even in the words of the book. It was in one of the pictures! That made me realize that writers need to pay attention to the pictures! We might even find that there are extra details there that can help us develop new opinions."

Notice again how you can ask some rhetorical questions, which get the children thinking, without actually calling on them, which would slow down your lesson.

Mercy Watson to the Rescue has many illustrations that enliven the story. We've chosen a favorite to return to—you'll know from reading the story aloud which pictures your students find particularly entrancing.

❖ **Name the teaching point.**

"Children, today I want to teach you that there are often parts of books that are told through the pictures. Writers, therefore, are always looking closely at the pictures in their books. Looking closely at the pictures sometimes allows you to see even more. And this new information can help you to develop new opinions."

TEACHING

Go back to a picture in the text and study it closely.

"Writers, let's look closely at a picture in *Mercy Watson* and see if there are parts that are told through the pictures, not the words. Let's also see if there are secrets or tiny details that are only told in the picture that give us new ideas."

I opened the book to page 4 and read aloud: "And so Mercy got out of her bed and went and got into bed with Mr. and Mrs. Watson." Then I showed the picture.

I waited a moment and then said, "I'm comparing the words and the pictures and . . . wait a minute! In the words, it just says Mercy got into bed with Mr. and Mrs. Watson. But in the picture, you can see that Mr. Watson keeps sleeping. He doesn't even notice that Mercy is there. Mrs. Watson cracks one eyelid and looks at Mercy under her eyelid! She has this smug little smile, as if she knows Mercy is there and is going to let her get away with it."

I turned back to the children. "Writers, Mrs. Watson spoils Mercy! The picture shows that she lets Mercy get into bed with her. So now, I've come up with *another* opinion about this book. Yesterday our letter was about how unusual we thought Mercy Watson was. Today, let's move on. Let's write about *another* opinion; that Mrs. Watson spoils Mercy. We'll work on a letter about this, and we'll explain how the picture shows it. But first let's look at some of the other pictures and see if there are other reasons Mercy seems spoiled. I seem to remember a picture with lots and lots of buttered toast." I flipped back through the book, finding the picture that showed a giant stack of buttered toast. "Yes. Here it is. Now let's quickly start a draft of our new letter. Can you think along with me about how this might go?"

I quickly jotted the beginning of my new letter.

> Dear Class 202,
>
> Did you ever know anyone who was spoiled? Well, I know a pig who is, and that is Mercy Watson! In <u>Mercy Watson to the Rescue</u>, Mercy is spoiled rotten by Mrs. Watson. She is spoiled because she has her own bed, a bed like a person would have, not a pet bed. I have never heard of that, a pet with a person bed. And, when she doesn't want to sleep in her very own person bed, Mrs. Watson even let's Mercy sleep in HER bed. I also think that Mrs. Watson spoils Mercy because she gives her huge plates of hot buttered toast, all the buttered toast that Mercy could ever want!

By referring to these as "secret details," you recruit your students to look with eagle eyes, motivating them to uncover additional details.

You can pause as you're writing, saying your ideas out loud, looking to children for confirmation, as if you are coauthoring. This drama makes children feel as if they share the writing process with you.

Debrief, highlighting your use of the pictures to help you develop and support a new opinion.

"Writers, do you see the way we used the pictures to come up with new opinions? And when we came up with the idea that Mercy is spoiled, we even found *more than one place in the book* to support it. That gave us a lot to write our letter about."

ACTIVE ENGAGEMENT

Give the children a chance to try this work in their own books.

"Now it's your turn to try. Why don't you and your partner open up *one* of the books you might want to write about and look at the pictures, or some of you might want to look at the picture books we've read aloud so far this year. They're in a pile right here too, as well as some copies of *Mercy Watson*."

Some children took picture books. Others picked up the books they had brought with them.

Zac and Eldin were huddled over the last page of our mentor text from our first unit, *Owl Moon*. "Pa is carrying the girl in this picture. I think that shows that she is still a little bit of a baby. I guess she got to go owling 'cause she was big—but not *that* big 'cause she still wants to be carried home," Zac said. Eldin added, "Yeah she looks kinda like a little kid in that picture." I interjected, "Hmm, so you are thinking that the picture is giving you a new opinion, the idea that she is still a little kid in some ways?" Zac and Eldin nodded. Before I left, I coached them to imagine the words of the letter. "So how would your letter start? 'Dear . . .'" As the children rehearsed the letter aloud, I moved on.

As the children notice parts that are told through the pictures, you can model how to grow their thinking into opinions. You can also channel them to particular parts of your read-aloud texts that you know will be productive.

Christopher and Bea had *Mr. Putter Bakes a Cake* open between them. "Look at Mr. Putter. He is really thinking. Like he has his hand on his face in that thinking way." Christopher acted it out, placing his hand around his chin just as Mr. Putter did in the picture. "You can see he is really thinking about it, not just saying 'Oh well, I don't have a pan. I can't bake the cake.'" Bea added, "Well he does think a lot, so the picture shows that." I leaned in, "Wow! So you two acted out the picture to help you think about it, and now you have an idea about the character! Now tell each other how that letter would sound."

Often just by saying "I wonder . . ." you can lead children from observation to analysis.

"Pinky's favorite stuffed animal wears pink too!" Sarah noticed. "It's the same pink and white striped shirt that is one of Pinky's favorites." When Sarah said this, I voiced over, asking, "Hmm, I wonder if that means clothes are really important to Pinky."

"There are pictures of Mercy all over the wall!" said James.

"Hmm, yes, that does feel like an important detail," I noted. "I wonder if that means The Watsons really adore Mercy?"

As I continued to listen into partnerships, the most common response I made was, "Oh, I bet you'll want to write about that!"

One of the more effective ways to get transference from partner conversations to kids' writing in any genre is to respond to their ideas with, "Oh, yes, you'll want to write about that!"

LINK

Reiterate that this strategy is one of several they have learned for generating ideas about books.

"Writers, we have a bunch of ways to get ideas for our writing, let's make a chart to help remind us of ways to uncover our opinions about books."

"You might pick one of these topics to write about, or you might have some other important opinions to share in a letter. And you also may want to pick a new book to write about. So many decisions you have to make! Before you go off to write, take a second and tell your partner what your writing plan is. What will you work on as a writer today?"

I gave partners a moment or two, then sent them off. "Off you go, writers. I can't wait to see how many letters you write today!"

Reminding the children that they can start a new letter can often increase the volume of writing in their folders.

Uncovering Our Opinions about Books

Writers can study . . .

- Characters
- Favorite parts
- Pictures

FIG. 3–1

Assessing and Teaching Your Writers Using the Opinion Writing Checklist

TODAY IS A GREAT DAY TO DO A LITTLE WHOLE-CLASS ASSESSMENT, to look around the room and ask, "What do *most* of my writers need?" "What do *some* of my writers need?" "What do just one or two or my writers need?" One way to go about gathering this information is to use the Opinion Writing Checklists from Grades 2 and 3. Holding the checklists and looking to see where children line up can be a quick way to organize groups and decide on teaching points. Using this information, you might focus today's small-group and conferring work on directing students toward new goals or helping them see ways to make their writing longer and stronger.

Using the checklists during writing time can also be a great way to see just what it is that children are doing, without getting lost in the details. The clear language of the checklists can give you concrete ways of naming what you see and then provide you with ideas about what might come next. Let's take a look at one student's piece as an example (see Figure 3–2).

FIG. 3–2 Elias's letter

Dear Reader,

The series Weird School is so weird (1) because in one book A.J. fell asleep in gym class and dreamed about Yoda hitting a Janke named Yoie but before they started fighting they were doing yoga. (2) They also did a math test under water. And also did a math test eating sweets and a police officer makes a gun with his hands and arrests all the teachers he sees. Don't you think that this is crazy? (3)

From, Elias

Looking at Other Features of a Book, Such as Titles, to Find More to Write About

"Writers, can I have your attention please?" I waited a moment for pens to be still and eyes to meet mine. "I was just talking to Audrey, and she had an idea for looking at other parts of the story besides the pictures. The letter Audrey is writing is about a book called *Henry and Mudge and the Forever Sea.* Audrey is writing about what the title might mean—Forever Sea. Isn't that clever?

"You might find it interesting to write about your title too, either the title of your book or the title of a chapter. Just for a minute, look at the title of your book, and try explaining what the title means to your partner. Why is the book called that? Turn and talk."

After a minute or two, I called the children back. "Writers, eyes up here. Audrey has reminded us that the pictures aren't the only part of the book that might have extra meaning. Good thinking about titles, Audrey! If any of you find other parts that have special meaning, make sure to alert us all so we can explore those ideas in our letters. While you get back to work I'm going to add 'Titles' to our chart of what we can study to uncover our opinions about books."

Here's how we might analyze this piece:

1. **Lead:** The writer names the text he is writing about and gives his opinion about the text. This writing is quite straightforward and does not yet appear to "hook" the reader.

2. **Transitions:** The writer uses *because* and *also* to connect his opinion to an example. His examples are evidence from the book to support the opinion. The writer gives multiple pieces of evidence for his opinion, not just offering one bit, but several bits. While the writer has an opinion and examples/evidence, he seems to have left out a real *reason*.

3. **Ending:** The ending provides closure, reminding the reader of the opinion that is discussed throughout the letter. There is not yet a thought or comment added to the opinion in this conclusion.

First, decide if the child is reaching toward second or third grade. Then to assess without spending hours dissecting each piece of student writing, you might choose one category from the second grade checklist and then peek over students' shoulders as they write, quickly looking to see what children are doing with this. You can keep a running list as you go. Looking at several children's writing with an eye toward one category can also help you to understand each point in that category better. You might find that there are a number of children like Elias who are stating an opinion and then jumping right to the evidence, without stopping to think about their reasons for their opinion. These writers might need to think about why their opinion is true. What makes the book weird/unusual/scary? If the group includes half or more of your class, this discovery will surely affect your whole-class minilessons in the days to come. If, however, just a handful of children seem to be doing this, then you can pull them into a small group right away and address using reasons in opinion writing.

Next, you might decide to choose another category from the third grade checklist and circle the room gathering information about what students are trying with that set of skills. Doing this quick assessment early on is a great way to look at what you have

planned for your teaching in the next couple of sessions and assess if it will meet the needs of your students or whether you need to adjust a bit—moving more quickly to keep up with children who seem to already do what you had planned to teach or slowing down to revisit skills with which your students might need more time. You may also want to see if there are a few children who need work with the same teaching point. These kinds of quick assessments are not meant to replace lengthier, more thoughtful and comprehensive assessments, but assessment is so important it can't wait until you have a long stretch of time or until the unit is near completion to find out how things are going. Remember, your students' work is the best way you can get feedback for your teaching, so treat it as such. Look for the places where your students need more support and also places where you can just let them take flight. (You can find these checklists in the online resources.) ✶

Opinion Writing Checklist

	Grade 2	NOT YET	STARTING TO	YES!	Grade 3	NOT YET	STARTING TO	YES!
	Structure				**Structure**			
Overall	I wrote my opinion or my likes and dislikes and gave reasons for my opinion.	☐	☐	☐	I told readers my opinion and ideas on a text or a topic and helped them understand my reasons.	☐	☐	☐
Lead	I wrote a beginning in which I not only gave my opinion, but also set readers up to expect that my writing would try to convince them of it.	☐	☐	☐	I wrote a beginning in which I not only set readers up to expect that this would be a piece of opinion writing, but also tried to hook them into caring about my opinion.	☐	☐	☐
Transitions	I connected parts of my piece using words such as *also*, *another*, and *because*.	☐	☐	☐	I connected my ideas and reasons with my examples using words such as *for example* and *because*. I connected one reason or example using words such as *also* and *another*.	☐	☐	☐
Ending	I wrote an ending in which I reminded readers of my opinion.	☐	☐	☐	I worked on an ending, perhaps a thought or comment related to my opinion.	☐	☐	☐
Organization	My piece had different parts; I wrote a lot of lines for each part.	☐	☐	☐	I wrote several reasons or examples of why readers should agree with my opinion and wrote at least several sentences about each reason.	☐	☐	☐
					I organized my information so that each part of my writing was mostly about one thing.	☐	☐	☐
	Development				**Development**			
Elaboration	I wrote at least two reasons and wrote at least a few sentences about each one.	☐	☐	☐	I not only named my reasons to support my opinion, but also wrote more about each one.	☐	☐	☐
Craft	I chose words that would make readers agree with my opinion.	☐	☐	☐	I not only told readers to believe me, but also wrote in ways that got them thinking or feeling in certain ways.	☐	☐	☐

Learning from Our Classmates' Strategies

Share how a student has invented another strategy for developing opinions.

"Writers, I'm so proud of you for finding all these secret details today, and because you are not waiting for me to teach you everything. You are inventing strategies. You figured out that the titles might be worth writing about, for instance. Well, Levi wrote about *another* part of his book. Listen to this part of Levi's letter." I read aloud (see Figure 3–3).

> Dear Reader, I really think Mr. Putter and Tabby Bake the Cake is a really good book. You should read it. Just take a look at the cover and you will realize that Mr. Putter is trying to bake a cake. There is something really funny on the cover too. Can you see that Tabby is in the pot watching Mr. Putter bake the cake? That is very funny, don't you think so? Tabby is always trying to get close to Mr. Putter. And can you see the details he put into that one broken egg? It reminded me of when me and my mom make scrambled eggs every morning. I think cracking the eggs is fun but Mr. Putter looks afraid.

"Writers, including the cover as one of the pictures in the book led Levi to the opinion that Mr. Putter is afraid to bake a cake! Give a thumbs up if the cover of your book might be worth writing about. Thank you Levi! Writers, add this strategy to those you're already using. You might write opinions about the characters, about favorite parts, about the pictures, about the meaning of the titles, and now maybe the cover! Let's add this idea to our chart, too. That will help you to work even more independently!"

Uncovering Our Opinions about Books

Writers can study . . .

- Characters
- Favorite parts
- Pictures
- Titles
- Covers

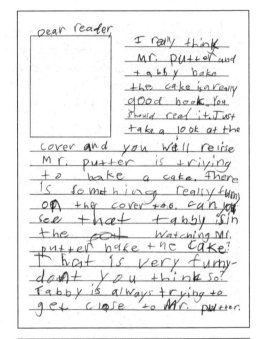

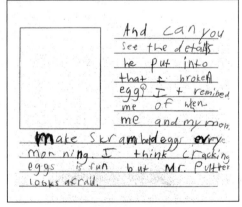

FIG. 3–3   Levi writes an opinion he developed by looking at the cover of his book.

Writers Make Their Letters about Books Even Better by Retelling Important Parts

NOW THAT YOUR WRITERS ARE writing letters about books, you'll want to shift their focus from *what* to write *about* to *how* to write *better*. They'll raise the level of their work by revising old letters and drafting new ones. Soon you'll also move some of the letters from book baskets and writing folders to a "Wall of Fame," so that writers can turn to mentor letters to get ideas for how to raise the level of their writing. This will help children throughout the entire unit.

Writers of any age can make their writing better by really explaining things to their reader. When writing about reading, that usually means retelling. If you teach your students to assume that their reader hasn't read the book they are writing about, they'll usually realize they need to explain more. They may need to explain more about the characters. They may need to explain how the book starts. They'll certainly have to explain important parts that they mention in their letters.

For this session, you may want to demonstrate by writing an opinion on a different text than your read-aloud text—because your students have all read that book, so no explanations are needed. You'll note that we demonstrate with a few sentences from books that children *might* know but that we haven't discussed in depth so far.

You'll also have an opportunity to return to the focus on partner work that you started a few sessions ago. Teaching students to not only talk as writers but to listen closely as writers is ongoing work. Explaining your writing—saying it out loud—is half the work of expressing it. Getting students to say more is one step toward getting them to write more. In this session, partners will rehearse their writing during the active engagement portion of the lesson, focusing on retelling parts of their stories related to their opinions. You already introduced linking words such as *because* in previous lessons. Now your students will also find *for example* helpful; a phrase you may have taught your students in reading workshop as well. "Poppleton is kind. For example, . . . " If you haven't, now is a good time to focus on some of those reading-writing connections, so that your students are supporting opinions about their books as readers as well as writers, giving examples.

IN THIS SESSION, you'll teach students that writers who write about books often need to retell part of the story in order to help their readers fully understand their opinion.

GETTING READY

- ✔ Sample sentences that leave out a needed retelling, either from student writing or the ones we use to demonstrate (see Connection)

- ✔ *Poppleton* by Cynthia Rylant or another text that your students might not all be familiar with (see Teaching)

- ✔ Books that students are writing about (see Active Engagement)

- ✔ Post-its and pen and writing folder (see Share)

- ✔ Chart paper and marker (see Share)

Writers Make Their Letters about Books Even Better by Retelling Important Parts

CONNECTION

Gather some intriguing sentences, ones that are sort of cliff hangers, and read them aloud to your writers.

"Writers, I've been reading some of your letters. They have me dying of curiosity. Listen to some of these sentences."

I read a few lines from letters, making my voice lift like a storyteller's.

> *Annie is really brave, especially when that Tyrannosaurus Rex is about to eat her! If it was me I'd hide under a rock.*

> *Poppleton is mean and angry. I can't believe he pointed the hose at Cherry Sue. It was awful what he did.*

> *The best part is when the talking toilets begin to chase the kids because it is so funny. "Yum, yum, eat 'em up!" I hope my toilet doesn't do that.*

I leaned forward as if on the edge of my seat. "If you're like me, children, I bet you're dying of curiosity—and maybe a little confused too. A *Tyrannosaurus rex*? Talking toilets?! What's going on here?"

❖ **Name the teaching point.**

"Writers, today I want to teach you that writers who write about books often need to retell part of the story to help their readers understand their opinion. If you don't do a little bit of retelling, your readers might be confused."

TEACHING

Demonstrate how to explain more to your reader by retelling important parts that are connected to your opinion. Return to one of the sentences you just read as an example.

"Let's go back to those sentences we just read, writers. They are such teasers! This time, let's try to do more explaining, so the reader will understand what we're talking about. I'll demonstrate. If you've read the same book, go ahead and

---

You can pull some "teaser" sentences from the letters in your classroom. Or steal a few of these, as it's doubtful children will track down your sources. If you are teaching this unit of study across the grade, you can imply that these came from various classrooms.

You'll note how even though you are demonstrating, these small phrases such as "go ahead and think about" or "you can think about" engage students' minds during the lesson, so they are working while you are working.

---

think about what you might say to explain. If you haven't, you can think about what questions you have and see how I answer them by retelling part of the story."

I picked up the list of sample sentences again. "Let's do this one, from Poppleton. I found it really confusing, because Poppleton is pretty much never mean. And yet this writer says he does something bad to Cherry Sue! Well, I found that book, and listen to how I might add an explanation by retelling part of the story."

Book in one hand and student writing in the other, I reread the sentence. "'Poppleton is mean and angry. I can't believe he pointed the hose at Cherry Sue. It was awful what he did.'

"Okay, I definitely need to explain how this happened. The reader will be asking, 'Poppleton? Really? What did he do to Cherry Sue?' So I might say . . . "

Slow down your demonstration, really showing what it looks like to recall important parts and retell them.

I paused as if thinking, and I also flipped through the pages as if looking. Then I said, slowly, "Poppleton is so mad when he soaks Cherry Sue. It all started when Cherry Sue kept bringing food over and shouting 'Yoo-hoo!' She did it again and again until finally Poppleton couldn't stand it anymore. He didn't know what to say, so he just suddenly turned the hose on her and soaked her! It was really funny, but also awful when he did that!"

I looked up at the children. "That would make a lot more sense to my readers, wouldn't it, children?" The children nodded. "Now my letter will be much better, because I retold part of the story. So now, even if my reader has never read Poppleton, he or she will know enough about the story to understand my opinion."

ACTIVE ENGAGEMENT

Invite your writers to do this work by first planning the opinion they'll write about today.

"Writers, I'm going to give you a chance to do this work. You can practice explaining really important information to your reader.

"Can you take a moment now, and first, think about what you are writing a letter about today? When you get to a new letter will you be writing an opinion about a character? About a favorite part? Opinions about the picture, title, or cover?" I pointed at the anchor chart to remind students. Put a thumb up in the air when you're ready to say an opinion that you'll write about in a letter today."

Next, prompt your writers to rehearse the part of the story they will retell, with a partner.

I waited a moment, then prompted, "Now, writers, you have your books at hand. Knowing what you want to write about, why don't you take a moment to think about which part of your story might be important to retell. If you need to

I try to show some of the pages as I develop my explanation, so children can see my thinking. One reason we use books with pictures for these demonstrations is they cue up the story quickly.

It's important to act as if coming up with ideas for writing is often no big deal. Otherwise children can become stalled, searching for the perfect idea, when they should be writing—and any idea will probably be okay. It's hard to get better if you're not writing, and it's easy to get better if you start quickly.

glance at your book to remind yourself, do so. Then, as soon as you're ready, turn and tell your partner what part you'll really want to explain to your reader."

As the children talked, I gathered some examples to share. Then I interrupted their conversations. "Writers, it sounds like you have solid plans. I heard Levi retell the part of *Magic Tree House* where Jack and Annie time travel and suddenly find themselves in front of a hungry dinosaur! And Petra was retelling the part of *Pinky and Rex* where Pinky has so many pink stuffed animals and fights with his sister over a new one they find in the store. Such good thinking. If Petra hadn't retold the part of the story where Pinky shows off all his pink animals, we wouldn't know why he wanted this one in the store so much."

LINK

Reiterate that explaining information to readers is always one way to write better, and remind students that talking and listening to a writing partner really helps with this work. Then send them off to write.

"Writers, whenever you are writing, one way to write even better is to really explain things to your reader. You seem like you're all energized to write, so off you go. But wait, hold on one more moment.

"I do want to give you one bit of feedback. I can tell your partner conversations are really helping you rehearse your writing. From now on, think about being a good listener as well as a good talker in those conversations. Just now, I saw you really listening for stuff that is confusing or that you'd like to know more about, and telling your writing partner to be sure to explain those parts. Keep it up."

Giving your students quick feedback keeps energy for hard work high.

Continuing to Teach from Information Gathered and Further Helping Writers with Retelling

IN THE PREVIOUS SESSION YOU COLLECTED a lot of information about your writers while looking at the Opinion Writing Checklist. You likely organized a number of small groups but worked with only one or two of these groups. Today you can pull more groups. Remember that in any small group children can revise and change letters they have already started and/or completed, and they can also start fresh with new letters. Take a look at your students' work to determine whether you need to encourage students to do one or the other. If the child has many pieces that show a strong effort and then just end quickly, you may decide to encourage her to add on. On the other hand, if a child has only one letter that has become long—and perhaps a bit unwieldy—you might encourage the child to start with something new. Remember, writing a number of pieces in each part of a unit will be useful to your students' writing development. Writing many pieces helps the child to repeatedly go through the process of getting an idea, turning it into writing, and then making it better. If you notice that a child is avoiding one or another step in that process, you will do well to focus your teaching on that missing step.

In addition to pulling groups you prepared yesterday, you may find that there are children who are not quite grasping the importance of retelling. These children are often

---

MID-WORKSHOP TEACHING   **Setting Readers Up to Understand the Big, Important Parts of Your Book**

"Writers, can I have your eyes please? I want to share a conversation I just had with Lily. Lily is writing a letter about the *Magic Tree House* book, *Haunted Castles on Hallows Eve*, and she jumped right in to start telling about how the *most interesting* thing in the story was this very cool poem in the book. And Lily did retell that one, interesting part. She told what happened and even put the poem right in her letter.

"Then Lily read the letter to her partner and he said, 'Wait I don't get it. Why is that happening? What's going on here? Why are these kids in a castle?'

"I was sitting right there and all three of us just had to laugh. It was so true! Lily just thought her reader would automatically know that the kids in *Magic Tree House* books time travel. But how would you know that if you hadn't read the book? We couldn't understand Lily's opinion about the letter because we needed to know just a little bit more about the whole book and what the story is about.

"So, Lily added on to her letter by starting with 'Dear Reader, I'm reading a *Magic Tree House* book about a brother and sister called Jack and Annie. The story is about when they travel in their treehouse back in time to a castle. One of the most interesting things in the story is . . .'

"Writers, can you see how just telling the reader a little bit about how the story starts or what it's mostly about helps the reader make sense of the rest of your letter? That means that sometimes retelling just a *part* isn't quite enough. You need to set up the book by introducing what it's mostly about, too. So Lily needed to say that Jack and Annie time travel. If I wrote about Nate the Great, I might write a little bit about how he's a detective who solves mysteries, or if I wrote a letter about Zack Files, I might add that Zack has weird things that happen to him with music."

Children nodded, and gave Lily a thumbs-up signal. "You might want to reread your letters and see if it would be helpful to add a little bit at the beginning to introduce the book to your reader. If so, add it now!"

---

lacking in the "Elaboration" section of the checklist and need extra support considering the ways they might support an idea clearly, completely, and cohesively. Consider my conference with Eldin.

I had begun my research with Eldin by simply peering over his shoulder and reading what was in front of him. He was signing his name to a newly completed letter (see Figure 4–1) that read:

Dear Reader,

I think Poppleton is a very nice and fun pig. In Poppleton Everyday, he is very funny, because he just keeps asking for more things and things. I guess he's not fun, but he is fun to read about. Also in Poppleton Everyday, I like when Hudson cuts the hole in his blanket and puts it over Poppleton's head, because then Poppleton looks like an alien. But I don't get how putting a tiny towel with a hole over your face helps that. Hudson says, "Now you will only see one tiny sky." But I don't get how that's gonna help him, but it did work! I guess Hudson has good ideas.

From,
Eldin

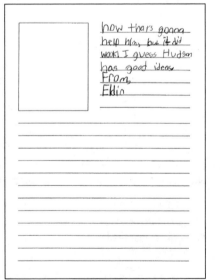

FIG. 4–1   Eldin's letter before revision, where his lack of retelling makes it hard to follow.

After reading this, it seemed clear to me that Eldin needed to understand that his reader might not know the stories he was writing about. But before I jumped in to do more work with retelling, I checked Eldin's folder to see if this was a pattern for him. Luckily, there were two other letters in the folder. Both were shorter than this one—I could see Eldin's growth in just these three pieces of writing—but neither had any retelling, making all three hard to follow. I sat down next to Eldin and started, as usual, with a compliment. "Wow, Eldin! I see you have just finished your third letter, and look at this." I laid his other two letters next to the letter he was working on now. "You have already written longer, and with more opinions and examples from the book!" Eldin touched his newest letter, and a smile crept onto his face.

"Yeah, you said we need an opinion, and I put one here. I also put examples from two parts of the book, and this is a really funny part with Poppleton sick looking at the stars." Eldin pointed at his work as he spoke.

"Hmm, that does sound funny, Eldin. These examples are really making me curious about the book. But can I tell you something?"

"Yeah."

"Well, I have to admit that I have never read this Poppleton book and I am a little confused. You see, it sounds really funny, but I don't know what is going on in the book, and that makes it hard for me to understand this part of the letter." I pointed to the part about Poppleton looking like an alien.

"Oh, yeah, Poppleton is looking at the stars. And Hudson loves it, but Poppleton is getting seasick. He is lying on the blanket and, you know, the sky is so big and deep. He feels sick!"

"Oh! So the sky is so big he feels sick looking at all of it at once? That makes so much more sense to me now. Now I get it!" Eldin smiled. "You know, Eldin, when writers write about books, sometimes their readers don't know the books, so it can be really helpful for the reader to tell a bit of the story to clue the reader in on what is happening. Do you think you can add a sentence or two that clues the reader in on what's happening, just like you just did for me?"

At first Eldin looked a little unsure, so I handed him a revision flap and asked him to retell again out loud. Once he had rehearsed orally, he then had an idea of what he would write. I waited as he wrote the retelling and taped it down, just to be sure he understood (see Figure 4–2). I then asked him to reread and look for any other places

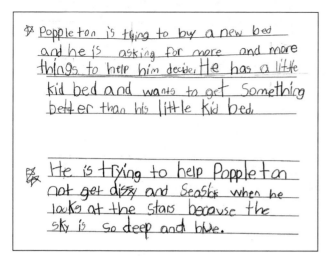

FIG. 4–2   Eldin uses strips to add retelling to his writing, thus clarifying his letter.

where a retelling might help. He decided to add one at the beginning of the letter too. Before I left, I again restated my teaching and reminded Eldin that this would help his reader to be excited and clear about the stories he was writing about. Finally, I made a note in my conferring notebook about checking in with Eldin on this and perhaps pulling him into a small group with other children who might need continued support with retelling, too.

Dear Reader,

I think Poppleton is a very nice and fun pig. In Poppleton Everyday, he is very funny because he just keeps asking for more things and things. Poppleton is trying to buy a new bed and he is asking for more and more things to help him decide. He has a little kid bed and he wants to get something better than his little kid bed. I guess he's not fun, but he is fun to read about. Also in Poppleton Everyday I like when Hudson cuts the hole in his blanket and puts it over Poppleton's head, because then Poppleton looks like an alien. But I don't get how putting a tiny towel with a hole over your face helps that. He is trying to help Poppleton not get dizzy and seasick when he looks at the stars because the sky is so deep and blue. Hudson says, "Now you will only see one tiny sky." But I don't get how that's gonna help him, but it did work! I guess Hudson has good ideas.

From,
Eldin

Using *For Example* to Introduce Text Evidence

Draw attention to the work that you saw students doing today adding retellings to their letters. Then explain to students that their retellings are a form of evidence and can be highlighted for readers by using the phrase *for example*.

"Writers, find a good place to stop in your writing and let's gather on the rug. Please bring your writing, some Post-its, and a pen."

When the children were seated, I reviewed a bit of what we had been working on. "Writers, it was very interesting today, walking around and seeing so many of you thinking about where you needed retelling to help your writing make more sense. Put a thumb up if you added some retelling today." Thumbs went up and I nodded.

"You know that it isn't enough to just say your ideas about books. You have to convince other people to believe you! And when you're trying to convince someone else, it helps to give evidence that proves your idea. We've been practicing this using the word *because*. So, we might say that Mercy is a special pig *because* she does unusual things, like sleeping in a bed.

"Sometimes it isn't enough to just list out some reasons and evidence, though. Your readers need you to give details! When they want to say more, writers can retell a bit of the story and use that as evidence. They find a place in their book that shows what they are trying to prove and then use the phrase *for example* to introduce it.

"Let me give you a quick demonstration using our Mercy Watson example from before. Instead of just saying 'Mercy is a special pig *because* she does unusual things like sleep in a bed,' I might say," and I jotted on chart paper as I modeled this for children.

> Mercy is a special pig <u>because</u> she does unusual things like sleep in a bed. <u>For example,</u>

I emphasized the use of the words *because* and *for example* for children, underlining them as I wrote to show the way that one expanded on another.

You may choose to slow this part of the share down by actually modeling this work with your shared text. You might reread, find a part to add for example *to, and then show how you think of the quick retell for the example and jot it down on the revision strip, finally taping it into the piece.*

<u>For example</u>, in the first scene, Mercy is getting tucked into bed by Mr. and Mrs. Watson. They make sure she is snug and cozy by wrapping the blankets around her. Then, they sing her a special lullaby and kiss her goodnight. Mercy sure is a special pig!

"Do you see what I did there? I gave my idea (that Mercy is a special pig), then I used *because* to add my reason. I didn't stop there, though! Next I added *for example* and retold a part of the story that proved my idea."

Help children transfer this work to their own writing.

"Take a moment with your partners now and try this out. You don't need to write the whole retelling now. Just use your Post-it to mark a spot where you can add *for example*, right after one of your reasons. Then you will know where to add a little retell that goes with your reason. Partner 1, you can share your writing first.

"Wow! Writers, so many of you are thinking about where a retelling might really help to prove your idea. You are adding evidence! Very impressive. Let's continue this work tomorrow."

You'll notice I am not saying that they must have an idea, supported by several reasons, and that each reason must have several examples to support it. This is the work of third and fourth grade, and while I'll support children who are ready to develop more essay-like pieces of writing, it is certainly not my goal for all the children. Instead, I hope to help children realize that they can support ideas with reasons and examples.

As children try this work, you can move among them, keeping an eye out for those who might need more support. As you assist them, you may want to consider whether the nudge right now is enough or whether you should gather them for small-group work tomorrow.

Keeping Audience in Mind

IN THIS SESSION, you'll teach students that writers write with a specific audience in mind, angling their writing toward their readers and writing as if they are talking to them.

GETTING READY

✔ Chart paper and marker, with the beginning of an opinion letter already written, the audience being a reader who is familiar with the touchstone text that you are using for the unit (see Teaching)

✔ A second version of the letter, written on chart paper, angled toward a reader who is unfamiliar with the touchstone text (see Active Engagement)

✔ Opinion Writing Checklist (see Conferring and Small-Group Work)

✔ Chart paper with the heading "Think About Your Reader" (see Share)

LETTER WRITING OFFERS A UNIQUE OPPORTUNITY for young writers to develop a sense of audience. After all, the letter you write to your grandmother about a book might be very different than the one you write to a close friend.

At this point in the unit, many of your writers will have addressed the majority of their letters to "Dear Reader," though hopefully some have written letters to specific people in their lives. Today offers you an opportunity to highlight the differences that come with writing to various kinds of audiences. Thinking of audience means picturing that particular person or group and then deciding how you might talk to that person—what vocabulary you might need to explain, what references you can make, and so on. We make conscious and unconscious decisions about this all the time. Teachers know that if they want to develop examples of character traits, if they use the example of Miss Piggy or Kermit, most American second-graders will not need more explanation about those characters. On the other hand, if you were to give opinions about these characters to second-graders in another country, you'd probably want to explain that Kermit is a talking frog—a particularly kind and nice talking frog—and that Miss Piggy is a fierce and not-so-nice talking pig.

Today you will help children picture a specific audience and the differences in the audiences they might address. With these differences comes choice. Will the writer include a retelling because the reader has not yet read the book? Will the writer write about a specific kind of book that this particular reader will really enjoy? Will the writer include certain details about the book to make the letter even more engaging and exciting for the chosen audience? Helping children to make these decisions thoughtfully raises the level of their work. As your students consider whether their reader will need a retell or whether they will include a certain detail or how they will engage the reader, they will be working hard to choose well from the many strategies you have already taught.

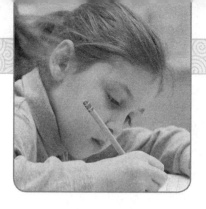

Keeping Audience in Mind

CONNECTION

Engage your students in a quick shared inquiry about where their letters should live.

"Writers, as I've been visiting our book baskets, I saw so many letters about so many books. These letters are really renewing my interest in books that have been sitting on our shelves all year! And I've seen you reading some of these letters before setting off to read these books yourself.

"It made me think that as we write more and more letters, we need to let these letters do their jobs in even bigger ways. We need to let the letters inspire other readers to read our favorite books or inspire readers who aren't even in this classroom! Let's think for a minute about where else these letters should live to do their jobs. We have already put them in the books themselves. We've put some around the classroom. But can they do more? Should you send them to partners or family members or friends? Should they go up on the walls to inspire other writers? Where should these letters live?" After a quiet pause for thinking, I said, "Tell your partner where you think your letters should live."

I listened in to be sure that we got at least two or three different ideas. Then I reconvened the class.

"Class, everyone has some smart ideas about where our letters can go. Let's share some."

Rimari started us off. "I want to put my letter in the Zack Files basket in our library. That is what we did first, and I want to do that again." I looked around, and children were nodding and adding, "Me too! I want to put mine in a basket."

Bea raised her voice to say, "Yeah, then we can keep reading each other's letters before we read the books!"

I held up a hand to stop more conversation for now. "Great! So one system is that you put your letters into the books or baskets. What else?"

"I want to send my letter to my cousin because I wrote it for him," Calder added.

"Who else would like to send their letter to a special reader?" I asked. Hands went up as voices from around the room proclaimed that they too had letters to mail. "Great! If your special reader is in school, you can hand-deliver your letters

By prompting students to propose venues for their letters, you'll not only boost engagement by granting students' choice, but you'll also remind writers of the purpose of this genre—directing their attention to audience.

to them. If that reader is outside of school, we'll have to find the address and use an envelope and stamp. And make sure to start your letter, Dear Susie or Dear Aunt Tabitha."

Then I added, "You know class, I was also thinking that putting a few letters on the wall might inspire us. We can have a selection of letters up, so that people can get ideas from each other's writing. What if I clear a little space on the wall for us to hang a few letters?" The children nodded.

Reiterate what has been said so far, and transition from the idea of where letters live to the idea of a specific audience.

"Great, so we can put some letters in the library, and some will be sent out to family and friends, and still others will be posted on the wall for inspiration. If you come up with other ideas for where our letters can live, just let me know!

"There's one more thing, though, writers. Now that you are addressing your letters to a specific audience, that means you can make your writing even better."

❖ **Name the teaching point.**

"Writers, today I want to teach you that you can write even stronger letters by picturing your audience and then writing with that person in mind. One way to do this is to think about whether your audience is a new reader or someone who has also read the book. Then, you write as if you were talking to that person."

TEACHING

Using your read-aloud text, engage your students in thinking about what a letter might sound like to someone who has already read the book. Emphasize how you think about what you would probably talk about if you were together.

"Let me show you what this looks like, writers. I think to myself, 'Am I writing to someone who already knows Mercy Watson? Like a friend or reading partner who has read the book too? Or am I writing to a new reader, who doesn't know anything about Mercy?'"

I paused for a second, then said, "I'm going to write a letter to my friend, Audra. I know she has read Mercy Watson many times. That means I don't need to explain who Mercy is or what happens in the story. Since she's read it so often too, it makes sense that I dive right into favorite parts. I know that's what I would do if I were talking with her. I'd start off with 'I think the best part is . . .'"

I picked up my marker and flipped to the chart paper on which I had written the start of a letter. "It might sound like . . ."

Don't underestimate the power of displaying student work across the unit. Posting a variety of examples highlight strategies and implicitly urge peers to take on this work, too.

Dear Audra,

I know you've read <u>Mercy Watson to the Rescue</u>, too. I think my very favorite part is when the Watsons think that Mercy has rescued them, because she really didn't go to the rescue. She was just looking for buttered toast, not the fire department! Wasn't that funny? I'd love to know your most favorite part too.

Another favorite part of mine is . . .

Reinforce the work you just did by saying it again as a series of steps.

I turned back to the children. "Writers, do you see how I first thought about who I was writing to? Second, I thought about whether or not this reader had read the book. Third, I pictured myself talking to this person, and explained the parts I would really talk about if we were together."

ACTIVE ENGAGEMENT

Give your students a chance to try this work, setting them up with a letter to someone who hasn't read the book.

"Now I'm going to give you a chance to try this work, writers. I'm going to put up the start of the same letter about Mercy, but this time, let's imagine I'm writing to my friend Gerritt, who *hasn't* read Mercy Watson and has never even heard about Mercy! Let's think what to add to make this letter even better."

I flipped the chart paper to a new letter, which started:

Dear Gerritt,

You should read <u>Mercy Watson to the Rescue</u>. My favorite part is when the Watsons think Mercy has rescued them.

"Writers, think for a moment now. We've spent a lot of time the last few days talking about how important it is to retell important parts and big ideas, to set up your reader to be able to understand your opinion. What would you need to explain to your reader, Gerritt, who is totally unfamiliar with Mercy Watson? Would you explain who Mercy is? Would you retell why the Watsons needed to be rescued in the first place? What more should we say in this letter?

"When you have an idea what you might want to explain or retell, turn and tell your partner what more you would add to this letter so that a reader who doesn't know this book would understand."

The children began talking. After they had spent a few moments hashing out the parts of this story that would be important to explain to a new reader, I pulled them back together.

Be sure to not only repeat back what you've just done in your demonstration, but to also name your process in a transferable way, helping students replicate the strategy in their own work.

Often you can tuck in implicit cues to help students get started, as if they were about to think of that same content themselves. Once they hear these possibilities, they're often better oriented to the thinking work you're expecting. Phrases such as "Would you say . . . " or "Maybe . . . " or "Perhaps you'd want to . . . " help students get started without making the prompting too heavy-handed.

"Writers, I like how you were thinking hard about what a new reader would need to know, and you were using everything you've learned so far about opinion writing and writing letters about books. Sam, for instance, was saying that he would explain who Mercy Watson was—how she lived in a house, was a pig, and so on. Grace wanted to retell the part of the story that comes before the rescue, so the reader would understand why the Watsons needed to be rescued at all. Christopher wanted to add more reasons why the reader should read *Mercy Watson*—what makes it such a great book."

LINK

Prepare students for independent work by giving them a few moments to decide on the specific audience they'll be addressing, considering how that choice will affect the content of their letter.

"Writers, some of you will be starting new letters today, while others of you will want to go back and revise old favorites. Before you head off to write, take a moment to prepare. Think about who you are writing to. Is it a reader in this class? Is it a family member or a friend? Then decide whether you think this person knows the book you're writing about, or if your reader doesn't know the book, and you need you to introduce the characters and the story."

The children thought for a moment. Then I said, "Writers, turn and tell your partner your plan for the day. How has the work we've just done affected your plans? What more will you say in your letters now that you're thinking about your audience? Remember, you can write as if you are talking right to that person!"

After writers had planned for a moment, I tapped shoulders, with an "Off you go. Get to writing while your energy is strong!"

It's sometimes helpful to insist that children do the thinking work you are describing "right now." Occasionally, a little bossiness helps make sure that students actually try what you say while it still makes sense to them. Otherwise, what you mean as a strategy they might take as an option, and ignore it and then actually forget it because they've never applied it independently. A link like this sets students up to develop a plan (which incorporates today's new learning), thus ensuring greater productivity during the workshop.

Drawing on Three Teaching Resources for Strong Writers

NOW THAT YOUR WRITERS ARE UP AND GOING—writing, adding, starting new pieces—you may find that you have a few children who have really taken off. (See Figure 5–1.) These are the kids who just "get it." They have chosen who to write to, they have books they are passionate about in their hands, and when you read their letters, you think, "What more is there to do here? These kids really have it!" Teachers of writing workshop quite often get this feeling, especially when we think back to the kinds of writing we made as kids. It doesn't even compare, does it? But just because your students are doing great work, doesn't mean you will simply leave them be. Just like you want to lift the level of your struggling writers, you'll want to teach your advanced writers to do more, too.

There are three great resources you can use to help you find teaching possibilities for your strongest writers. One of these resources is the writers themselves. If one child in the group thought about the audience as a way to get a new idea for a letter, you might share this strategy with others, nudging them to include parts of the book that reader would especially like. Or perhaps another writer thought about younger readers who might want to read his book and then wrote a letter to parents about whether the book was appropriate for little kids or whether the book should be skipped; this, too, is a strategy worth sharing. You may find that some of these writers are elaborating by adding three of four examples from the text. You can point that out to the group and then challenge them to do the same. The idea here is not to assign new writing to these children, but to allow their creativity and excitement to wear off on one another.

The second resource for helping strong writers can be the rest of the unit. Remember that when some children are really picking up pace in their writing, often all they need is a little teaching that you have planned for later. You can look over some of the lessons to come and ask, "Might these kids be ready for that right now?" I often find that trying a bit of teaching with a small group that I intend to present to the whole group later allows me to practice that teaching, too. So maybe you will pull a small group and teach the share for Session 9, teaching children to uncover life lessons in

---

MID-WORKSHOP TEACHING **Spoiler Alert! Don't Give Away the Ending—Leave Them Hanging!**

"Writers, can I have your eyes for a minute? I wanted to share with you something that Dante did with his writing to really draw in his audience. Listen to this part of Dante's letter." I read aloud.

> In Chapter 4 it gets even worse. It says it right in the chapter heading. THE WORST THING THAT EVER HAPPENED. Now Pinky may not be the best speller in the class anymore because of that kid Anthony. But that's not as bad as what happens next. He should have asked to go to the bathroom. He doesn't want to take a break from that spelling bee, so . . . [I read the ellipse as "dot, dot, dot."] I'm not going to tell you the rest—just read the book!

Everyone laughed out loud. "Hey you cut yourself off!" Lily called out.

"Lily, you said it! Writers, I bet you noticed just what Lily did. Dante got you excited by telling you about the plot and the character, but then he just cut himself off. He wrote 'Dot, dot, dot. I'm not going to tell you the rest—just read the book!' Dante, by keeping the ending a secret, you made us all want to read the book. Plus, you didn't ruin the ending for your audience.

"It would be fun to try it just like Dante did. First, you can tell an exciting part, then you can use a dot, dot, dot and invite your reader to read the book to find out."

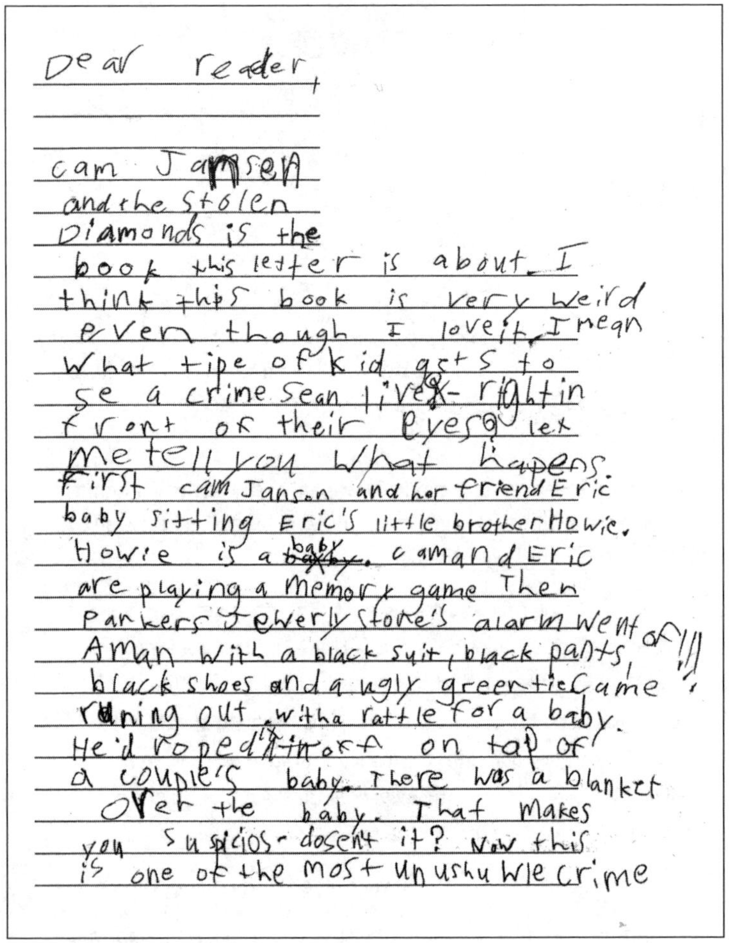

Dear reader,

cam Janson
and the stolen
Diamonds is the
book this letter is about. I
think this book is very weird
even though I love it. I mean
What tipe of kid gets to
se a crime sean lives right in
front of their eyes lex
me tell you what hapens.
First cam Janson and her friend Eric
baby sitting Eric's little brother Howie.
Howie is a baby. cam and Eric
are playing a memory game Then
Parkers jewerly store's alarm went of!!!
A man with a black syit, black pants,
black shoes and a ugly green tie came
runing out with a rattle for a baby.
He'd roped it in of on top of
a couple's baby. There was a blanket
over the baby. That makes
you suspicios dosen't it? Now this
is one of the most unushuwle crime

FIG. 5–1 Jude states an opinion and then fills his reader in with a detailed retelling of the plot. He sprinkles the retelling with questions directed at the reader.

a story and write about them. Or maybe you will encourage these kids to do some of the work of Session 8, in which writers learn to engage in close reading of a text.

Finally, the Opinion Writing Checklist can be a great resource once again. This is easy enough to use because it lays second grade beside third grade, immediately showing you the ways a writer might progress along a trajectory of skills. For instance, when considering the overall organization of an opinion piece, a second-grade writer is asked to write "at least two reasons" and write "a sentence or two about each one." Third-graders, on the other hand, must write "several reasons or examples," with several sentences about each reason. Furthermore, there is an expectation that third-graders have begun to organize their information into paragraphs or sections.

For the children who are ready, you might consider pulling small groups around organization and elaboration, teaching them to first develop several reasons to support their idea, then teaching them to write several sentences to support each reason. Later, you might teach them that writers use paragraphs to group information and signal that a new reason or example is coming.

Keeping pace with these strong writers can give you a lot of ideas for whole-class teaching possibilities, so don't just leave them be!

More Ways to Think about Audience

Retell some of the work you saw children doing with audience.

"Writers, you have been thinking so much about your audience today! Let's share some of what you tried out to draw in your audience! Bring your writing to the rug!"

I waited until everyone was settled and then started. "Writers, as I moved around the room today I saw and heard so many writers thinking about their audience. I saw Grace writing a letter to her friend and including details about her favorite part of a book she hopes her friend will read. I heard Audrey reading a part of her letter to her partner to make sure it made sense, even to someone who had not read the book. And we all heard how Dante cut himself off in his letter—not telling the ending. That made his writing really exciting, but it also meant that his reader wouldn't be mad that he gave away the ending of his book. Give a thumbs up if you did something to help or to excite your readers today." Lots of thumbs went up.

Start an audience chart as children share their work with a partner.

"Writers, take a moment right now to find a place in your writing where you were really thinking about your reader. Maybe you did something like Grace or Levi or Dante did." I paused so children could look through their writing. "Maybe you did something else that you think will let your reader know that you want them to love your letter and love your book or that this letter is especially for them." I paused again, while children looked through their writing.

"Let's start a chart that will help us remember our readers as we write our letters." I flipped over the chart paper and revealed a page that read: Think About Your Reader!

"Turn and tell your partner what you did to care about your reader that might go on this chart." As the children chatted I listened in and started to add to the chart. Most of the children had done the three things we had mentioned already, but a few added other fun ideas. Elias, for example, read the following to his partner: "Reader, if you like funny stuff and crazy characters, you'll love *My Weird School*."

After a few minutes I called the class back together, and we read over the chart, which now looked like this.

"So, writers, anytime you are writing about books, these are good ways to show your readers that you care about them."

I make a point here, and often, of listing out some of the work I observe during writing time. I hope to help writers feel "seen" in the workshop and to make writers aware of each other's work.

FIG. 5–2

Using a Checklist to Set Goals for Ourselves as Writers

Dear Teachers,

This session ends Bend I. Tomorrow, and throughout Bend II, you will help children raise the level of their letter writing by teaching them ways to write longer, stronger, and more in-depth about books. Before this next step, however, we recommend asking children to step back, reflect, and take on the important work of self-assessment.

Because you have used the checklists before, and they are familiar to both you and your children, we imagine you'll find it easy enough to author the smaller details of this session. We recommend that you begin by reminding students of all they have come to know about self-assessing and using checklists, and then ask them to study their own writing, develop clear goals, and create action plans for growth.

One of the most engaging ways to start a minilesson is by celebrating all that the children have learned and tried so far. Of course, celebration is the exact tone that you will want here, since this session will end with a party of sorts.

MINILESSON

You might start by announcing that today is the big day. You can tell them that at the end of writing workshop the whole class will work together to get these letters out into the world. Invite the kids to imagine the classroom abuzz with some children posting their letters on the wall so they can inspire others and some tucking their letters into lovely envelopes and then slipping them into book bins where readers will find them as they choose books. Still others will get a chaperone to take them to the mailbox at the end of the block, where they can post their letters to family and friends.

Once the children are excited, ready to jump up and get to all the fun, you can remind them that there is one step left. "We don't just send our writing out into the world," you might say. "We make sure that it includes our very best work first!" And on this note you can harness up all that energy toward the work of final revisions and edits. This will be the ideal moment to gesture toward a chart of the checklist and offer up the teaching point,

"Today I want to teach you that when writers are ready to share their writing, they give it one last read, looking for ways to make it even better. They use all they have learned *ever*," and you might point at the checklist here, "to make their writing the best it can be!"

If you choose to take this tack, you might begin with a shared reading of the Opinion Writing Checklist (available in the online resources), giving children the opportunity to turn, talk, and process the various criteria they'll be self-assessing. Then, transition into your teaching by demonstrating how you read through your writing, looking for places where you have, and have not, done various things on the checklist. As you do so, remember to include the children. Perhaps you will ask questions such as, "Did I do that?" and then answer those questions yourself, even as your students offer their thoughts, too. You may choose to make changes right there on the spot, adding a flap or a page to fit the extra writing. Or you may choose to use a Post-it that marks the place where you will make a change later. If you use a Post-it, show the children how you write down a note about what you will add, so that you don't forget when it is time to add it. Either way, using these revision and editing tools as you demonstrate will reinforce the "construction" aspect of revision and editing for children.

During the active engagement, you can give the children an opportunity to try this in their own writing. Set them up to read over the student-facing checklist, then hold it side by side with one of their own letters. Perhaps you will even read the checklist to them and then ask, "Which of these do you think might help your writing? Partner 2, will you say what you think you will add and then read your writing to Partner 1 and see if you can find a spot to add it or fix it up?" As children work together, you might listen in, coaching partners to make suggestions for more revisions and edits. Then you can have partners switch roles, with Partner 1 now voicing a needed change and Partner 2 helping to find the perfect place for it.

Another possibility for the active engagement is to do this twice, first asking children to practice using the checklist off of the class writing and then turning their attention to their own writing. This provides an extra layer of support, especially when we think our teaching will be a particular challenge for the children. Since your students have been revising and editing all year, this will not likely be the case today, but only you can know which parts of the process require extra scaffolds.

Before you send the children off to work, you will likely remind them that today they will want to work hard to make many of their letters better—fixing up one and then moving to the next. Remind them that at the end of the workshop these letters will go out into the world, and they want them to reflect their very best thinking!

CONFERRING AND SMALL-GROUP WORK

Because it is early in the unit, you may not have interrupted your children to focus them on spelling and punctuation in an effort to keep them writing and trying new work. Today is the day to remind them that if others are to read their writing, it needs to be easy to read. Perhaps you will choose to look at the "How did I make my writing easy to read?" portion of the checklist and pull small groups of children who need work on one or another of the skills listed there. It will be helpful to keep the demonstration part of these small groups short—perhaps simply reminding the children how to locate a part that needs fixing up—and then

FIG. 6–1   Rimari's published letter shows his effort.

spend the rest of your time coaching children as they work through editing their pieces. Once you have one group working, you can pull another and then perhaps another, moving from group to group coaching the children's editing processes. Remember, self-editing goes a long way. You want your students to be able to find their own errors and then fix them, not wait around passively while you point out everything that needs work. Also, don't forget that if some children are able to check off everything on the checklist without a single edit, then you will want to look at the third-grade portion of the checklist to offer those students constructive feedback that pushes them to aim higher.

MID-WORKSHOP TEACHING

Use today's mid-workshop teaching to reinforce positive revision and editing practices. Rather than one interruption, you might decide to provide several quick coaching voiceovers, spread out across the children's independent work time. This is a way to keep momentum going.

You'll certainly want to find and compliment children who keep themselves working for the entire period. "Writers, I'm sorry to interrupt," you might say, "but I wanted to point out something smart that Christopher just did. He was revising and editing one of his letters and then realized that he was done. Instead of just sitting there, Christopher took out another letter and started revising that one! Be sure to follow Christopher's lead and keep yourself writing the entire period."

You might also highlight the fact that several children are using the word wall and punctuation charts to make sure their writing is easy to read. "It's important to use all the tools in the classroom to help you edit," you'll remind.

SHARE

Though we are only through Bend I, you'll want to celebrate the work children have done thus far. You can choose any number of ways to do this, big or small.

You might choose to call your students to the meeting area with all the letters they are going to share. Maybe you will encourage them to put them in piles based on the destinations—one pile for letters to go on the wall, another for letters that will live in book bins, and another for letters that need addresses so they can be mailed. Once the writing is sorted, you might organize children into little centers—some working at a table with stamps and envelopes and the addresses they brought in; some with plastic sleeves in addition to envelopes—ready to slide in the letters that will live in book bins; and still another situated near the bulletin board where letters will be stapled to the wall for inspiration. The children can work at one station for a while, readying their letters, and then move to the next station, where they will ready a different letter.

You may choose to invite parents for this bonanza, sending kids out to the mailbox to send letters with a parent chaperone, or you may choose to have this be a smaller celebration (after all, we are only one third of the way through the unit!)—a "just us" celebration. Whatever you decide, have fun with it!

Enjoy!

Shanna, Ali, and Liz

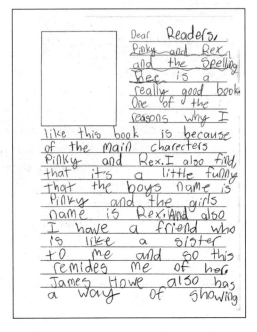

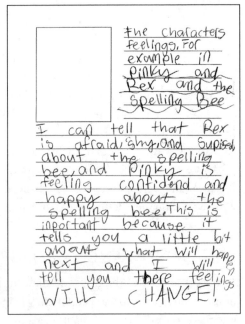

FIG. 6–2 Audrey's finished piece reflects her thinking about characters and an appreciation for author James Howe. She remembers not to give away the ending.

Writing about More than One Part of a Book

IN THIS SESSION, you'll teach students that one way writers make their letter writing stronger is by writing opinions about more than one part of the book and planning for the different parts of their letter before drafting.

GETTING READY

✔ "Make It Stronger, Longer, and More Convincing" chart (see Connection and Share)

✔ Multiple pages of letter-writing paper stapled together to create a letter-writing booklet (see Teaching). Stock your writing center with these booklets as well.

✔ *Pinky and Rex and the Bully* by James Howe or another touchstone text for this bend (see Teaching)

✔ "Uncovering Our Opinions about Books" chart (see Teaching)

✔ Chart paper and marker (see Share)

I N THIS BEND OF THE UNIT, you'll dive back into letter writing with the goal of helping children raise the level of their opinion writing through deeper analysis of texts and the use of more sophisticated elaborative techniques. Dive with excitement. Act as if this is going to be fabulous. Don't let a trill of nervousness seep out anywhere, even if in your secret heart you are thinking of little James, who is still only writing a few sentences. It's okay. You'll teach him to elaborate a bit more in this bend, turning those three sentences into six or seven or even eight. So often, when we are in classrooms where the teacher says that the kids are finding a certain kind of writing "really hard," we'll ask, "I wonder where they picked that feeling up?"

Young writers are tremendously susceptible to our own attitude about writing. So don't think, "This will be hard." Think, "This will be great! What a fantastic and beautiful task! We are going to write letters that are stronger and longer and smarter than the ones we just sent out into the world!"

You'll want to remind children that writing about multiple aspects of a topic is not new. They have planned for, drafted, and revised numerous informational books in their years as writers. In opinion writing, they have written reviews about their favorite movies or games. They have written to family and friends, sharing with them the best place in town to go for a cupcake or why to avoid the restaurant down the block—the one that serves French fries that are soggy and way too salty.

As this bend progresses, you'll teach children to write long about *one* idea, incorporating textual evidence and their own thinking to build an argument. Today, however, you'll start them off writing more by encouraging them to write long about a variety of *places* in their book. A very concrete way to do this is to present children with multipage booklets for their letters. Your students are accustomed to writing across pages, allowing themselves plenty of space to grow their ideas. In this session, you will bring this idea forward into letter writing.

Writing about More than One Part of a Book

CONNECTION

Welcome children to the new bend by praising the work they've already done. Invite your writers to recall what they already know about getting started with writing, and encourage them to think about what it looks like when they do their best.

"Writers, what a fantastic celebration we had yesterday. Just look at our wall of letters, and think about all the letters we sent out in the mail! I'm also noticing a ton of envelopes in the baskets in our classroom library; I bet those will be super helpful when you are looking for books for reading workshop. Our opinions about books are out for the world to see!

"Now, writers, we are going to keep writing about books. It's clear that you all have so much to say about the books you know and love. But I don't think writing teeny, tiny letters will be enough for us anymore, do you? You know way too much! Instead, I thought I'd teach you some strategies for writing longer, more grown-up letters about books. Do you feel ready for that?" Children nodded across the meeting area.

"Before we start today, let's spend some time thinking about what we know about writing strong letters. What have we learned that might help us now, as we write longer letters? Think for a moment. What do you already know how to do? Put a thumb up when you have an idea."

I waited until thumbs were in the air.

"Go ahead, turn and tell your partner your idea about something important you might do when you are writing letters today. I'll listen in and try to capture what you say."

Gather your children's ideas on a chart and then share them, capturing the major lessons you hope they took from Bend I.

As the children talked, I moved around with my clipboard. After a moment, I gathered their attention.

"Writers, what I really liked about your conversations is that you thought long and hard about what you learned in the first bend of our unit *and* what you've learned in prior units. I've started a chart for us that I'm sure we'll be able to add to in the next couple of days."

I try to tuck in praise for students' accomplishments so that the tone of the workshop celebrates students' voices as writers.

This kind of inquiry during the connection moves children into higher levels of agency and transference. You demonstrate that you expect them to carry their learning forward—and that you trust that they know stuff. It helps to emphasize not just "what they know about x," but "what they know about doing x really well."

FIG. 7–1

> Make It Stronger, Longer, and More Convincing
>
> - Introduce the book.
> - Write your opinion.
> - Give reasons—use BECAUSE.
> - Give evidence from the book—use FOR EXAMPLE.
> - Talk to your audience.

❖ **Name the teaching point.**

"Today, I want to teach you that when writers want to write *more*, one way they get started is by planning. They take a minute to plan for what will go in each part of their letter, remembering all the different parts of a book they can write about."

TEACHING

Invite students to recall some of the ways they developed opinions about books from Bend I. Explain that they have graduated to a point where they can write about more than one opinion in a single letter.

"Writers, let's give this a try together. Often, when writers are getting started with a longer letter, they imagine the different parts their letter will have. It's a bit like imagining the chapters in an informational book. In fact, I made us some letter booklets to help us do just that." I held up the new paper choice, fanning through the page. "Using this letter booklet, you can make a plan for a few ideas or opinions that you have about a book and then put each opinion on a different page, just like making chapters in information books.

"Let's try this with our book, *Pinky and Rex and the Bully*. Each part or section of our letter can explain an opinion, and we already know lots of different places we can stop and have opinions when reading!" I revealed the chart from Bend I, listing the parts of books that often spur opinions.

"Let's imagine that we are writing a long letter about *Pinky and Rex and the Bully*. What are some different parts of the book we might write about? What are some opinions we have? Turn and talk to your partner."

You will want to choose a book your children know and love. You might continue modeling using Mercy Watson *or, as we decided to, switch to another book the children have heard read aloud and know well. The important thing is that children know the book well enough to be able to practice these strategies alongside you.*

> **Uncovering Our Opinions about Books**
>
> Writers can study . . .
>
> - Characters
> - Favorite parts
> - Pictures
> - Covers
> - Titles

I listened in for a moment and then called the students back. "Okay, writers, we have a lot of opinions we could write about. I heard some opinions about the character," I pointed to the first bullet on the chart, "about how Pinky is different than other kids and how Kevin is a mean bully. A part of our letter could definitely be about the characters in the book! And a lot of you think that the illustrations in this book are so important, because they give information that the words leave out! Maybe we could write a section of our letter on that.

"Now watch how I plan a couple of these parts. I'm picturing how our letter might go. First, I'm going to write a bit about how Pinky is different than other kids." I pointed to the first page of the letter booklet to show where I would write that idea. "I bet I can fill almost all of this page writing all the ways that Pinky is different! Next," now I touched the second page of the booklet, "I'll write about how Kevin is a bully. That's two sections! Let's see, I could also write a new section about how important the illustrations are to the book." I touched the third page of the booklet. "Wow, that would be a three-page letter!"

Debrief by walking students through the steps you took to plan your new letter.

"Do you see how I did that? I planned a longer letter by imagining a few different parts it might have and by putting each of those parts on a new page. I got ideas for those parts by using our chart, 'Uncovering Our Opinions about Books.' Now, when I go to write my letter, I can push myself to write a whole lot about each opinion, using everything I know about good letter writing."

ACTIVE ENGAGEMENT

Invite your writers to keep going with the work you started together, coming up with more opinions they might write about.

"You can do this, too. So far, we've brainstormed three different parts our letter might have. Go ahead and turn and talk to your partner. Can you come up with a fourth opinion we might write about? You can use our chart if it's helpful."

FIG. 7–2

You'll notice that I've intentionally set students up to think about opinions, not just parts. Getting ideas into the "air" is often really helpful when students are getting started.

Call the children back together, sharing some of what you heard.

I listened in and then called the children back together to share their ideas. "Writers, you have so many opinions about *Pinky and Rex and the Bully*. I heard Eldin and his partner talking about how they could write about Mrs. Morgan. Their opinion is that Mrs. Morgan is a very wise character. Rimari and Dante want to write about their favorite part—the first chapter. Their idea is that Pinky is embarrassed about being saved by a grandma!

"Look at how much we know! We definitely know enough to write a nice, long letter with many parts."

LINK

Ask your children to plan for the sections of their own letters before heading off to work independently.

"Writers, I bet you know enough to plan for two or even three parts of your letter. Before you leave the meeting area, why don't you try starting this plan. What will be the first opinion you'll write about? How about the second? Can you think of a third? Once you feel like you have a good plan, go off and start writing."

You might decide to give each student their own small booklet, to touch each page and plan their letters across the pages. Planning across pages is not a new strategy for students at this point in the year, so the tactile practice may not be necessary. However, you know your students best, and if you think your students will benefit from this added practice, feel free to hand out blank booklets for students to plan with.

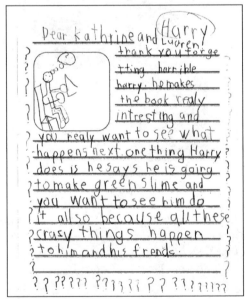
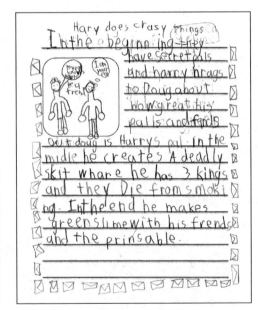

Harry: Dear Katherine and Lauren, Thank you for getting Horrible Harry. He makes the book really interesting and you really want to see what happens next. One thing Harry does is he says he is going to make green slime and you want to see him do it also because all the crazy things happen to him and his friends.

"Harry does crazy things": In the beginning they have secret pals and Harry brags to Doug about how great his pal is and finds out Doug is Harry's pal. In the middle he creates a deadly skit where he has 3 kings and they die from smoking. In the end he makes green slime with his friends and the principal.

Cool Things Happen: In the deadly skit there is three kings Harry, Doug and Song Lee and 3 angels Ida, Mary and Sidney. In secret pals each kid picks a name from a jar and whoever they get that's their secret pals. And when Harry and Song Lee make green slime Harry asks Song Lee for the ingredients and she gives him them. Sincerely, Eli

FIG. 7–3   Eli plans for his three sections, jotting keywords at the top of each page, before writing.

Supporting Writers in Paragraphing

Y OUR WRITERS WILL FIND BOOKLETS INCREDIBLY HELPFUL when attempting to elaborate on their ideas and create sections for their letters. There is nothing like the turn of a page to say to a reader (and a writer!) "I'm on to a new idea." You may find that some students are ready to graduate from writing across pages, however, and you'll want to pull these children into a small group to teach them how to compose expository paragraphs.

Noah, Petra, and Levi had all written one section of their letters and were about to begin a second section, on the second page of their booklets. I seized this opportunity to teach each of them how to paragraph. "Noah, Petra, Levi—I pulled you together because I think it is time you graduated from booklets to something more grown-up. How would you feel if I taught you a bit about something called paragraphing?" They each smiled, pleased that they had done strong work and were ready to move onto bigger things.

I put Noah's piece of writing between the three of them (see Figure 7–4), using it to begin my teaching. "Noah, will you tell Petra, Levi, and me a bit about what you were planning to do next?"

"I wrote about how Mr. and Mrs. Twit are mean people. Next," and at this he turned to the second page of his booklet, "I am going to write about my favorite part, when Mrs. Twit puts her glass eyeball in Mr. Twit's drink."

"Gross!" The other children and I looked at each other in disgust. "Wow, those sound like some interesting characters, Noah!" I stopped teasing, taking on a more serious tone. "What I want to teach the three of you is that grown-up writers don't turn to a new page every time they have a new idea. Instead, they fill a whole page with their writing, using paragraphs to tell their reader when one section is done and a new one is beginning. So, Noah, you can start writing about your favorite part of the book right here, on this sheet of paper." I tapped the sheet where he'd written his first body

MID-WORKSHOP TEACHING
Jotting Notes at the Top of Each Page to Hold Your Idea

"Writers, find a good place to pause for a moment. I want to give you a tip." I waited for a moment while pens stopped and eyes met mine. "Now that we are writing longer letters and planning for more parts, you may find that you are forgetting your plans. Put a thumb up if that has happened to you." A few thumbs went up, along with some nervous giggles. "Well, Eli just figured out a quick and easy way to fix that. Remember earlier when you made your plan and touched each page, telling where each part would go? Well, instead of just *saying* what each section will be, you can write it. You can jot a few words at the top of your page to help you remember what each section will be about. This is quick, and when your plan is written down, you can't forget it! Take a moment now and say your plan again, but this time jot a few words on each page to remind you what you will write in each part."

paragraph. The children looked at me, nodding their heads, but clearly not quite grasping what I was saying yet.

"Let me show you what I mean." I took out a piece of paper on which I'd already written one paragraph. "I wrote one paragraph here, about how Pinky is a different kind of kid. I'm ready to go onto my next section, which will be about Kevin the bully. But," I emphasized the *but*, making sure Noah, Petra, and Levi were with me, "I don't need to use a second piece of paper! Instead, I can make a new paragraph and start writing about Kevin right here, on this page. Let me show you."

I modeled skipping to the next blank line and making a small indent with my finger. "I'm going to skip to a new line and make a big space, called an indent. This way my writer will know that I finished talking about Pinky and am moving onto a new topic." Then, I began writing the first line of my new section in the next paragraph.

"Why don't you three give this a try? Instead of starting a second page of writing, see if you can make a new paragraph and write your next section right under the first." I coached them as they skipped a line, made a small indent and then began writing their second paragraph.

Once I was sure they had gotten the swing of it, I wrapped up my teaching. "Noah, Petra, Levi." I looked at them each in turn. "What do you think you'll do when you are ready to write about your *third* section?"

"Start a new paragraph!" said Petra. I reiterated the teaching. "That's right. You'll skip to the next line, make a little indent so your reader knows a new part is starting, and then begin writing. You'll only need a second piece of paper when you fill up this first one!" I sent the children off with a new paper choice: plain, lined paper.

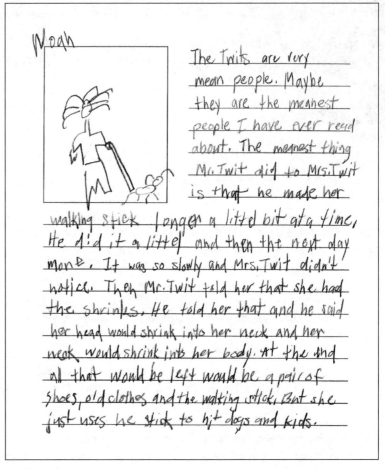

FIG. 7–4 An excerpt from Noah's letter that shows he is ready to learn about paragraphing.

Using Literary Language

Work with students to create a chart listing domain-specific words for writing about books. Encourage them to incorporate these words into their letters.

"Writers, will you join me on the rug with your writing folders, pens, and a clipboard?" As the children gathered, I started a quick chart. I titled it "JUICY Story Words." Many children read the title as I wrote it and started to chat. We already had a chart titled "JUICY Words" in the classroom. The "JUICY Words" chart was overflowing with words children collected from read-aloud and independent reading that they thought were especially interesting and that they wanted to use in conversation and writing. The children were clearly curious about this new "juicy" chart.

"Writers, this whole school year we have been collecting words we like and want to use and putting them on our juicy word wall. How many of you think that when you use the words from that wall you sound smarter and more grown-up?" Lots of hand went up. "We also have some words that we have collected that go with our science work, right? That's sort of like a juicy science words chart." The children agreed, and a few pointed to the force and motion words that were still up from our last science unit. "How do you feel when you use those words?" The children said they felt smarter and more grown-up using those words too.

"Well, today I want to teach you that books and stories have special words, too. These are the words that experts use when they talk and write about books. And when we use these special words, not only do we sound smart and grown-up, but we also make it easier for our readers to understand our ideas! What kind of words do you think belong on this chart?" I waited a moment to see if any of the children would start the list right away. When they didn't, I started to write a few words on the chart to get their thoughts flowing. "Juicy Story Words: Character, Setting."

After just these two words children started calling out other words we had used to talk about our books. Soon the list included more.

FIG. 7–5

"Wow, we know a lot of juicy story words. Using these words will help make your writing sound clearer and fancier! Right now, pick up your writing and reread it. Where can you take out an ordinary word and put in one of these juicy story words? Your writing will sound so grown-up when readers see these words in there!"

As children worked, I added today's new strategies to the chart we began in the minilesson.

After a few minutes I stopped the revisions. "Writers, isn't it cool how changing just a few words in your writing can make it sound so much smarter?" The children agreed. "I am going to hang our new 'Juicy Story Words' chart right next to our juicy words chart so you can use it every day to make your writing stronger."

FIG. 7–6

Depending on what you've taught children, this list may look a bit different. If children offer little to no words for the list, you might use this opportunity to introduce them to a few new words, broadening their vocabulary and then making sure to incorporate those words into book conversations in the weeks ahead.

We use the term juicy because it is one that our children are familiar with. You'll want to adapt the language of this lesson to fit the work your children have already done. Perhaps you simply have a word wall and explain to the students that you will soon be adding a story word wall to the bulletin board. Perhaps you refer to domain-specific language as "expert" language or "technical" vocabulary. Some teachers use the adjective sparkling for literacy language. The wording itself does not matter; it's the notion that writers use specific, expert language.

Reading Closely to Generate More Writing

I F YOU'VE EVER WRITTEN ABOUT A BOOK, you'll recall how while you were writing, you seemed to notice the smallest details in the story, ones that you might otherwise have overlooked. Think back to high school or college, when you were writing literary essays, and you would notice tiny details in a poem or a play or a novel. You would reread that poem or play again and again, searching for details and reveling in their discovery. Writers who write about books almost always read more closely.

That work, of noticing details and thinking about their meaning, is the work of close reading, which many educators think is some of the most significant work of world-class reading standards. Those standards ask students to pay attention to the language and craft of texts, noticing how these two entities come together to create the ideas, themes, and lessons in a story. Your children can do this close reading work in the writing workshop as well as reading, as they learn to mull over and ponder the details of the books they are writing about.

IN THIS SESSION, you'll teach students that when writing about reading, writers read closely and carefully, paying attention to details that others may pass over. They use these details to grow new ideas.

GETTING READY

✔ "Uncovering Our Opinions about Books" chart (see Teaching)

✔ *Pinky and Rex and the Bully* or other touchstone text (see Teaching and Active Engagement)

✔ Your own writing booklet that you began planning in Session 7 (see Teaching)

✔ Chart paper and marker (see Share)

"Writers who write about books almost always read more closely."

In today's session, you will teach children to carefully and purposefully reread their texts, paying attention to details they may have originally passed by, mulling over the meaning of those details, and then using what they notice to generate new ideas about the story. This work will set the stage for tomorrow's lesson, when you'll teach children to reread in search of text-based evidence to support their opinions.

Reading Closely to Generate More Writing

CONNECTION

Use an example to illustrate the importance of close reading.

"Writers, last night I was rereading one of my favorite books: *Nate the Great and the Phony Clue*. In this mystery, Nate has to figure out who left a torn piece of paper with the word *VITA* on his doorstep. Nate's not the only one who tries to figure out these mysteries. He has friends who often try to help. But Nate is always the one who solves the mystery!" I pulled myself forward in my chair and leaned toward the children. "I realized that Nate is such a great detective because he *looks closely* at things. Nate notices all the little things that other people miss. For instance, in this one part, he studies a tree in his friend Rosamond's yard and finds a torn piece of paper hanging from a twig. No one else had seen it! In another part, he found a little, tiny scrap of paper in the sewer, floating in some water.

"The reason I'm telling you about these things is because you can learn something important from Nate. Nate finds things because he looks closely and carefully. As writers, we need to do the same."

♣ **Name the teaching point.**

"Today I want to teach you that when writing about reading, writers don't just read quickly over the parts they are writing about. Instead, they are wide-awake readers, reading closely and paying attention to little details that others might pass by. Then, they use these details to grow new ideas and to write longer, more detailed letters."

TEACHING

Demonstrate by looking back at an important part of the touchstone text. Highlight the fact that you pause to attend closely to what's in the text, saying or writing what you notice.

"When you are trying to be like a detective and grow new ideas about your book, it's important to reread. You can look back at all the places we've been studying together: the cover, characters, favorite parts, pictures, and more." I pointed to our class chart listing places writers can find ideas for their opinions.

"Let's look back at *Pinky and Rex and the Bully* and see what kinds of new things we can notice. Make sure your minds are wide-awake so that you don't miss a detail!"

♦ COACHING

You will always want to draw your children in to your teaching. Notice how I draw them in here by connecting our work as writers to the work of one of the children's favorite characters. The detective analogy will serve children well as they learn to read closely and carefully.

Uncovering Our Opinions about Books

Writers can study . . .

- Characters
- Favorite parts
- Pictures
- Titles
- Covers
- Lessons

I read aloud a portion of Chapter 5, "Hard Choices," knowing this bit of text would provide ample opportunities for analysis. I noticed that the children were listening, but none had put a thumb up to signal that some of the details might be worth thinking about. I stopped reading and said, "I don't see many thumbs up yet. I'm the same as you; sometimes I just want to let the story flow over me. But to grow big ideas about a text, it helps to pause often and to push yourselves to notice important details."

I began to read aloud a second time. "Let's be like detectives and notice details we didn't see before. Think along with me. Each of you, pick out something important." This time I read a bit more slowly. I knew the part about Pinky confiding in his stuffed animal Pretzel, sharing his misgivings about not being able to play with Rex, was full of rich details. I finished the section and looked up at the group.

"I always thought this part was so sad," I began. "It's like Pinky has to give up everything he loves just so he won't get teased. But let me look a bit closer. What details am I noticing now, as I reread, that I missed the first time around?" I scrunched up my face and looked back at the book, visibly thinking hard. "Are you guys noticing any new details?"

The children clamored to their knees, wanting to add what they were noticing. "I'm thinking what you are, I bet," I said. "I didn't really stop to notice that Pinky talks to his stuffed animals. That's a new detail. Let's see what else." I went back to thinking. "Even though his stuffed animals can't talk back, Pinky makes Pretzel's head move from side to side, to show that he doesn't understand why Pinky can't play with girls anymore."

Make it clear that noticing is not enough. Instead, writers need to ask, "What new ideas does this give me?"

"Just noticing something new isn't enough, though. I need to take what I notice and ask, 'What new ideas does this give me?'" I returned to thinking. "Well, I'm starting to realize that bullies have made Pinky very unsure of himself. He is so unsure that he is going to end his friendship with Rex. It's like he doesn't know what to do, and he just needs someone (even Pretzel!) to give him advice or agree with him!"

I jotted my new idea at the top of the next page in my letter booklet. My jot read, "The bullies make Pinky unsure of himself." "I bet I could write a whole lot about all the ways Pinky is showing he is unsure of himself."

Debrief by explaining to students how you noticed new details and incorporated them into your planning.

"Writers, do you notice the way that I reread part of my story, pushed myself to notice new details, and then used those details to plan a new part to my letter? I had even more to say because I reread and paid attention to even the smallest detail."

If you want students to read closely and notice more in the text, you'll need to model how to read slowly and methodically. Many second-graders read quickly through their books. Showing them how to slow down will be part of the teaching here.

Take students step by step through this new work. If you think students need more support you might name out the steps as you go. "Okay, so FIRST I . . . , then I . . . , now I need to. . . ."

ACTIVE ENGAGEMENT

Give children an opportunity to try the same work using the touchstone text.

"Now it is your turn to give it a try. Let's try looking at an illustration this time. How about the picture that begins Chapter 5? We've seen it before, when we read the story, but now let's go back to it and look again, really pushing ourselves to see more." I showed children the small illustration of Pinky's stuffed animals. "First, let's be like detectives and notice as many details as we can in this picture. Then, we'll ask whether any of those details help us to have new ideas. Go ahead and tell your partner what you notice when you look closely." I gave the children a minute to talk before calling them back together.

"Let me share some of what I am hearing. Dante and Rimari were noticing that the dinosaur has a diaper on. Thumbs up if you saw the same thing." Thumbs flew into the air. "I also heard you saying that the stuffed animals have lots of pink on them and that they are dressed in cute little outfits, like a sweater and a dress.

"Now ask yourself, 'What ideas are these new details giving me?'" I coached in as children talked, offering a few prompts to bolster their thinking. "This makes me think . . . " And then, "The idea I'm having is . . . " When I pulled the students back together, I asked Eliza to share what she and her partner had discussed.

"Well," Eliza began confidently, "we were thinking that Pinky takes really good care of his stuffed animals. Like he put a diaper on the dinosaur and a sweater on Pretzel." Eliza shared her observation but stopped short of giving her idea—her opinion.

"So what does that make you think?" I asked. "I think this means he is caring." Eliza smiled. "Very nice. Writers, do you see how Eliza and her partner took the little details they were noticing and grew a bigger idea—that Pinky is caring? I bet they could write a whole page about all the ways that Pinky is caring."

LINK

Remind students that they should be working toward the goal of writing more about their opinions, and that close reading of their books can give them more ideas to write about. Prompt them to think back to all the strategies they've learned to make their writing powerful.

"Remember that your biggest goal today is to write, write, write. Whenever you are looking for something new to write about, you can do some close reading. Go back and look closely and carefully at a part of the book, notice details you didn't see before, and then ask yourself, 'What new ideas do these details give me?' Take a minute and make a plan for the writing work you'll do when you go off today. What will you do first? What will you do second? When you have a plan, turn and tell your partner." As I listened in, I heard most children saying they'd reread closely for new ideas. Seizing the opportunity to reinforce repertoire, I added, "And don't forget, you don't just have today's strategy to help you write. You can use *everything* you've ever learned as a writer to make these the best letters ever."

Teaching children to read closely is a process, and one that will not be accomplished in a day. Don't fret if you find your young writers focusing on details that are inconsequential ("I see buttons on Nate's coat. I never noticed that before!") Rest assured that you are instilling a habit of mind in your children—namely, the process of close and analytical reading—that will take some time to develop.

You'll want to emphasize that noticing details this way often comes from rereading and revisiting parts of a text. We can learn to review our reading (literally re-see/see more) to find more to say as writers.

Notice that as I name out what the children have done, I add in that next *they might write a "whole page!" This is not accidental—I am setting my expectations high!*

Linking Details and Ideas

YOU CAN PREDICT THAT AS YOUR CHILDREN VENTURE into the world of close reading, some will be apt to notice small, inconsequential details that do not relate to any larger ideas or themes. Praise the fact that the children have embraced close reading, and plan for some conferences and small groups that will help them make something more out of the details they accumulate.

I pulled up next to Sarah, who had written the following:

> When Pinky and Rex were on the way to school Pinky started talking about this spelling test (you should pay close attention to this part). "What test?" said Rex. "You know the spelling Bee." Rex was really scared.

"Sarah," I began, "look at all the close reading you've been doing! Tell me a bit about what you've discovered."

"Well," Sarah said, "I said a little part here," she pointed to her letter, "about how my reader should pay close attention to the part where Pinky and Rex are walking to school. When I went back and reread, I noticed new things, like that Rex was really scared about the spelling test. Her face looks really scared."

Before I went on to my teaching point, I wanted to praise the work Sarah had already done, so that I could link it to what I was about to teach her. "Ah, so you were able to reread and see more. Fabulous. I'm wondering, Sarah, if these details are giving you any new ideas. Noticing details is very important, but it's even more important that you let those details spark new ideas you can write about." Sarah and I returned to the scene where Pinky and Rex were walking to school and reread a bit. As she read, I gave her a few tips. "One thing that is helpful is to read a line or two and then say, 'This makes me think . . .' Then, read another line or two and say, 'This makes me think . . . ' You can keep doing this until you come up with a great idea."

MID-WORKSHOP TEACHING
Writers Use What They Notice to Spark New Ideas

"Writers, many of you are rethinking details as you reread your books. For instance, Eldin noticed that Stink is named Stink but that he doesn't smell bad! But here's the really cool thing Eldin did. He didn't just stop there. Instead, he pushed himself to ask questions and have some new ideas about what he was noticing. He wondered if maybe Stink has that name because he used to smell bad. Or maybe it's just a funny name someone gave him. Or, maybe he has a stinky personality!

"When you notice something important in your book, don't just sit back and relax. Instead, do some hard thinking. Come up with smart new ideas. These new ideas might even become pages. Eldin is thinking he might write one called 'Stink—the Cool Kid Who Doesn't Stink.'

"If you need some extra help, try some of these phrases to get you started:

- This makes me think . . .
- The thought I have about this is . . .
- I wonder why . . . ?
- What is important here?

As Sarah reached the part of the story where Pinky reassures Rex by telling her she knows more about dinosaurs, her eyes lit up. "I have an idea. This makes me think that Pinky is a really good friend!" she said.

I complimented Sarah on her ability to not just notice details, but to link those details to bigger ideas. She added onto her writing to incorporate her new thinking (see Figure 8–1 on the following page).

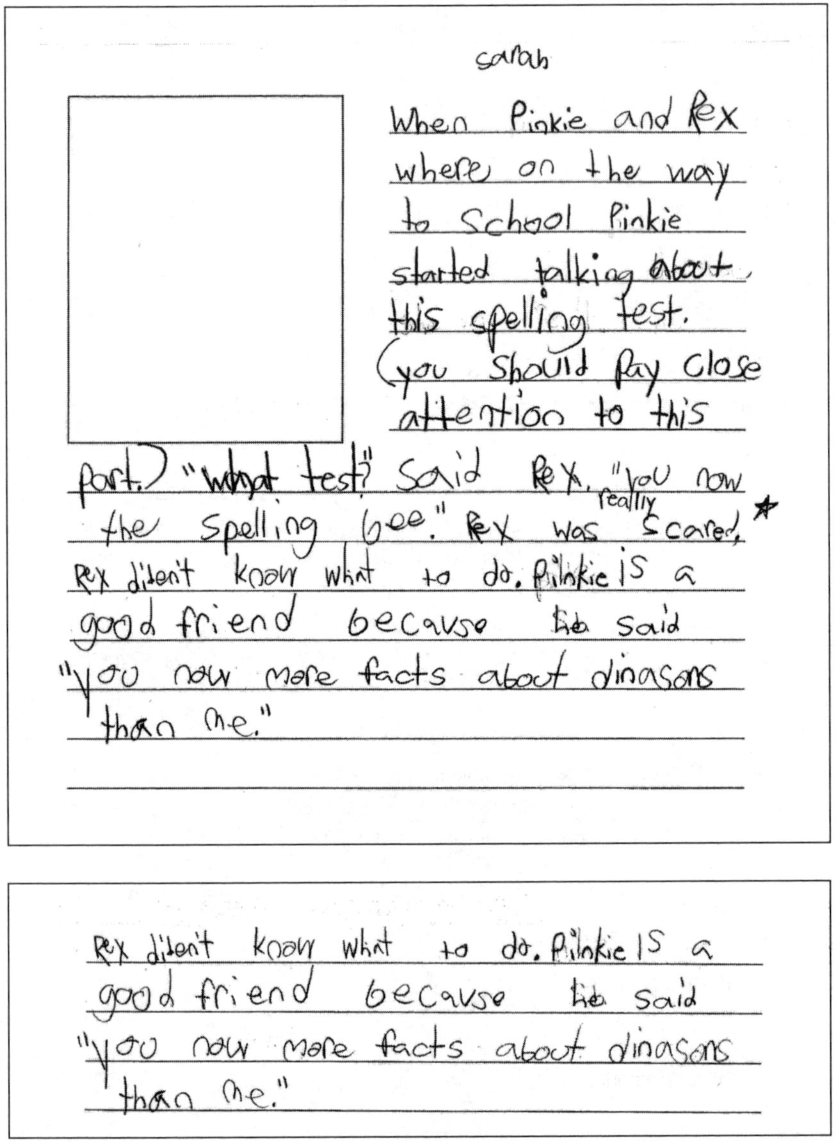

sarah

When Pinkie and Rex where on the way to School Pinkie started talking about this spelling test. (you Should pay close attention to this part.) "what test?" Said Rex. "you now the spelling bee." Rex was really Scared. ★ Rex diden't know what to do. Pilnkie IS a good friend because Lila Said "you now more facts about dinasons than me."

Rex diden't know what to do. Pilnkie IS a good friend because Lila Said "you now more facts about dinasons than me."

FIG. 8–1 Sarah adds onto her letter to show her new idea.

Other students, like Grace, may have identified a big idea but struggle to pull precise, supportive details from the text as evidence (see Figure 8–2). With these children you'll want to start with the idea and teach them to go in search of the evidence.

In this instance, you'll want to teach the child to hold her idea in mind (for example, the idea that Pinky and Rex is a book about friendship) and read closely for precise, specific parts of the text that prove this. Then, teach children like Grace to use all they know about paraphrasing to cite a specific portion of the text as evidence.

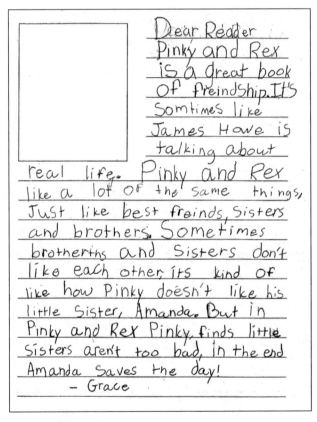

Dear Reader
Pinky and Rex is a great book of freindship. It's Somtimes like James Howe is talking about real life. Pinky and Rex like a lot of the same things, Just like best freinds, Sisters and brothers. Sometimes brotherihs and Sisters don't like each other, its kind of like how Pinky doesn't like his little Sister, Amanda. But in Pinky and Rex Pinky, finds little Sisters aren't too bad, in the end Amanda Saves the day!
   – Grace

FIG. 8–2 Grace identifies a theme in *Pinky and Rex*.

Having Books at Hand to Inspire Writing

Encourage your writers to gather their favorite books so they'll have them at hand to inspire them.

When all the children were gathered on the rug, I began. "Writers, I want to remind you that when you are finished writing about one book, you can start a new letter about a new book. Many of you have written a whole lot about one book, and now it is time to write something new. And you know that having your books beside you really helps you write. Today I saw some of you refer to the book to spell the title and the author's name correctly. Thumbs up if you did that." Some thumbs went up. "That's very wise.

"I also noticed children looking through their books to remember specific parts of the story so they could retell them." I motioned for children to indicate if they had done that too. Many had. "And many of you tried looking at your books closely, noticing little details you had passed by before. Turn and tell your partner other reasons to refer to the actual book as you write."

As the children talked, I listened in and jotted some reasons on a chart.

"Wow, you have a lot of reasons to look at your books! These are all fantastic!

"Writers, it seems that you all agree that having your books nearby when you write will be a big advantage. But a little problem came up today. Some of you wanted to move on to write about a new book, but when you looked around the room you realized it was not in your book baggy—or in our library. Let's make plans for finding the books we need. Think for a moment about the next two or three books you will write about. Put up a finger for each.

"When I send you off from the meeting area, I'll give you a few minutes to gather some books for tomorrow's workshop. This way, when you are ready to move onto a new letter, you won't have to go searching for a book to write about! And remember, when you wonder what to do with those books, you can look at the chart we just made."

FIG. 8–3

The share is a great time to set children up for the next day's lesson. By finding materials today, children will have more time for writing tomorrow.

Gathering More Evidence to Support Each of Our Opinions

IN THIS SESSION, you'll teach students that when supporting opinions about a text, writers look for multiple pieces of evidence to support each idea.

GETTING READY

✔ Your own writing about the touchstone text, enlarged on chart paper (see Teaching)

✔ *Pinky and Rex and the Bully* or other touchstone text (see Teaching)

✔ An excerpt from *Pinky and Rex and the Bully*, enlarged for students to see (see Active Engagement)

✔ "Make It Stronger, Longer, and More Convincing" chart (see Link)

✔ "Helpful Linking Words" chart (see Mid-Workshop Teaching)

✔ Chart paper and marker (see Share)

✔ "Uncovering Our Opinions about Books" chart (see Share)

MORE, MORE, MORE. It will be a few years before your writers reach the age, maturity, and skill where the focus of their revision will be to cut their writing. Before that stage are the many years when what they need to do is write more. More explanation. More elaboration. More description.

Since you have just opened the wide world of research up to your students, you will likely see kids with books in hand, scanning, jotting, and talking about all the great ideas they get as they comb through their books. By now, many of your students will have written a letter or two with several sections for each. Many of your students will have written a section, then moved on to the next, written a section, then moved on to the next. Adding more sections is a great way to add volume to any piece of writing, but it is only one way. I often tell children that there are "three kinds of *more*" in writing. I say, "You can write *more, more, more*. The first kind of more is writing more letters, the second kind of more is writing more parts or sections in one letter, and the third is writing more in each section of your letter." This last kind of more is what you will teach children to do today.

This is one helpful way to talk about types of volume with seven-year-olds. In fact, these three kinds of more represent varying levels of sophistication. One way to think of it is to think back to college. Likely, in your 101 courses you wrote five or six five-page papers, while in your graduate-level courses you probably wrote one or two twenty- to thirty-page papers. The longer the piece, the more the writer is elaborating on one topic. And the longer it is, the more sophisticated the ideas or arguments must be.

One reason why writers get better from writing more may be that what they think and say is so, so much more than they write. It's as if their minds and mouths work at such greater velocity than their hands can move the pencil. Sometimes, you can literally see their stamina flag as they write. They begin to shake their hands. They get up to go to the bathroom. They sharpen their pencils. Those writers are physically tired.

Other times, though, children simply stop after saying a very little bit about something, when they could, in fact, probably say more if pushed. So push them. Or better yet, teach your writers to push themselves. Anyone who ever got better at anything did so by doing it a lot. Sometimes simply marking an *x* at the bottom of the page, setting a goal for where they will write to, can be what it takes. Have them make chapters that are three pages each, instead of one. Teach them to encourage each other. "That's a fascinating opinion!" is something a writer loves to hear. "I can't wait to read what you have to say about that," is another great partner phrase.

"Anyone who ever got better at anything did so by doing it a lot."

When your children do begin to write long about one section of their letter, such as writing a lot about the character or the plot or the place or one little favorite part, celebrate along the way. Colored stars, smiley faces, and other hoopla are all to the good. We remember being in a writing workshop at Teachers College with Roy Peter Clarke, the prize-winning journalist, as he conducted a writing exercise. Just after asking a room full of teachers to write for five straight minutes from some simple prompt, he had everyone in the room hold their notebooks up in the air. "Look around!" he crowed. "Look how much you wrote. You, there, in the third row. You're on the second page! You, there, you're about to flip the page!" Everyone glowed. It reminded us that getting a lot of writing done, fast and furious, as Roy called it, can be a very good thing.

Gather More Evidence to Support Each of Our Opinions

CONNECTION

Congratulate children on the close reading work they did yesterday.

"Writers, yesterday you did a lot of detective work. You were like a whole class filled with Nate the Greats, looking closely and finding clues in your books to spark new ideas and opinions for your writing. Put a thumb up if you found a clue in your books yesterday that you turned into a whole new part or even a whole new page of writing." Thumbs popped up and children looked around, noting all the children who had tried this work. "The kind of detective work you did yesterday really helped to add pages to your writing. Congratulations!" Many children patted themselves on the back.

"Adding whole new parts or opinions to your letter is great, but it is not the only way that writers write more. Once you have an opinion and even a detail to go with it, you don't just stop there. You can make your writing even better by supporting each of your opinions with *more* details and evidence from your book. After all, you're writing letters that go across pages now, and each page has a new part or opinion.

"Think of it this way: when Nate the Great gets a new idea about who committed a crime and he finds one clue to go with it, he doesn't just say, 'That's it. I'm done!' and then sit back and eat some pancakes. *No way.* He does further investigation, he gets more evidence, to prove that the new suspect must be guilty, right?" The children nodded. "Well, that is what opinion writers do, too. Opinion writers think of their opinions, and then they reread their books to look for more and more and more evidence to back up, or prove, each of their opinions."

❖ **Name the teaching point.**

"Today, I want to teach you that after developing opinions about a book, writers search for many pieces of evidence to support each of their opinions."

You'll notice the progression of work we are doing with children in this bend. First, we sought to help them elaborate on their ideas by writing more opinions, about more parts of the book. Now, we are honing in on one part of that writing (one opinion) and teaching children to elaborate by adding details and evidence.

TEACHING

Let students know that you are aware that they are noticing details and using them to come up with an opinion. But now, they need to take it to the next level and search for even more details to support each of their opinions.

"You spent yesterday noticing details and then letting those details spark great ideas and opinions about the books you are reading. Each new opinion is becoming a different section for your letter, and because of this, many of you have two-, three-, even four-page letters!

"It's not enough, though, to support only one of these opinions! Instead, you need to hold each of your opinions in your mind and then go in search of lots of evidence that support each one."

Demonstrate taking an idea or opinion from a section of a letter and returning to a book to collect related details and evidence.

"Let me show you what I mean. Yesterday we added a new section to our letter about the idea that Pinky is unsure of himself. I wrote a bit about how that part of our letter could go." I unveiled a chart with a bit of this writing on it.

> The third-grade bully, Kevin, makes Pinky unsure of himself. He calls Pinky a sissy and says that he is like a girl. Pinky feels so unsure of himself that he decides he can't be friends with Rex anymore!

"I focused in on the idea that Pinky is becoming unsure of himself, and I even gave a detail to prove it." I pointed to and reread the line about Pinky planning to end his friendship with Rex.

"That detail is a great example of how Pinky is unsure of himself, but if I really want to prove that this is true, I have to include *lots* of strong details. My reader needs more evidence!

"This is going to require some more rereading and detective work! I think it might be time to grab my magnifying glass!" I pretended to hold up a magnifying glass as I opened *Pinky and Rex*. The children giggled.

I looked through the book, visibly thinking as I did. "Hmm, are there any other details that prove Pinky is unsure of himself?

"I know." I showed the children the cover of the book. "On the cover is a picture of Pinky with his soccer ball. I remember this part of the story. Kevin took Pinky's soccer ball and started making fun of him for being a girl. Pinky didn't stand up for himself, and afterward he wondered if he really *was* a girl. Let me add this new piece of evidence to my letter." I picked up a marker and began adding on.

Notice that I have kept this writing short, including only my opinion and a detail to support it. This is purposeful. I don't want to overwhelm the children with a lot of writing that is unrelated to today's minilesson. Instead, I want to offer a clear, accessible example that all can learn from.

If you do this right, children will be clamoring to their knees with answers. Hold them off just a bit longer so you can continue modeling.

The third-grade bully, Kevin, makes Pinky unsure of himself. For example, he calls Pinky a sissy and says that he is like a girl. Pinky feels so unsure of himself that he decides he can't be friends with Rex anymore! Another example of when Pinky feels unsure of himself is when he is playing soccer and Kevin takes his soccer ball. Kevin teases Pinky and tells him that he is a girl. Pinky doesn't stand up for himself. He even starts to wonder if he IS a girl.

Debrief, describing the process you followed to gather more details and evidence from the text.

I put my marker down, debriefing the moves I'd made for the children. "Writers, do you see what I just did there? I wanted to prove that Pinky is unsure of himself, but I only had one teeny, tiny detail to show it. So, I went back to the book and looked for more evidence to support my idea. Once I found a second part that showed Pinky is unsure, I added it onto my letter. I made sure that opinion was supported by lots of evidence. Now we need to do the same with each opinion in the letter."

ACTIVE ENGAGEMENT

Ask children to join you in supporting a new opinion.

"Will you help me now?" Pinky being unsure of himself isn't the only opinion this letter shares. In this other part, we need lots of evidence to show that Pinky has parents who are very supportive. I revealed a chart-sized excerpt from *Pinky and Rex* and gestured for the children to hold up their pretend magnifying glasses. Then, I began reading.

> That night after dinner, Pinky was helping his father clean up. "Is it bad that I like pink?" he asked.
>
> "Of course not," his father said. "Pink has always been your favorite color."
>
> "Yeah, but now that I'm seven maybe I should like a different color."

"It's important that we pause and ask ourselves, 'Could any of this go with our idea?' Is the dad being supportive? What, specifically, is he doing that is supportive?" The children raised their hands, dying to chime in, but I continued reading on, hoping to give them a bit more evidence to grab onto.

> "What does being seven have to do with it?"
>
> Pinky put down his dish towel and slumped into a chair. Finally, he said, "Maybe you shouldn't call me Pinky anymore."
>
> "When you were little, we called you Billy," his father said.
>
> Pinky thought for a long time. Then he said, "From now on, I'm Billy."

When I was done reading, I turned back to the children. "Think for a moment. Is there any evidence here to support the idea that Pinky's dad is supportive? When you have an idea, turn and talk to your partner."

I model the use of transitions (For example, also) in my demonstration today, but I do not make it the main focus of my teaching. In this way, it is a bit of a tucked tip. It's important to make choices as you plan your lessons. So as not to muck up your teaching with hundreds of tips, decide what you will teach and what you will leave for later. During the mid-workshop teaching, I will draw students' attention specifically to the use of transitional words and phrases.

When students try this work themselves, they will often be able to rattle off a few details from memory. It's important for them to jot these down before they go on a journey looking for more. You might consider giving children Post-its on which they can jot their first thoughts before going back to reread.

I had chosen an excerpt from Chapter 4, "Billy," when Pinky was helping his father clean up after dinner and questioning his choice of pink as a favorite color. Pink had always been his favorite color, but now, with recent events at school, he was reconsidering. I knew this passage was chock-full of evidence that showed his father's support.

Small details in your language help children see how they are adding to their skills. Yesterday, you taught children to reread to gather more evidence. Today, you add on that writers need to do this work for each opinion as part of their writing.

As I circled around the rug I coached the children, helping them to identify small, specific parts of this scene they could use as evidence.

I called the children back together, and we added the new evidence onto a new page of our letter. Soon we had a piece that looked like this.

> Even though Pinky feels unsure of himself sometimes, he is lucky enough to have a dad who is supportive. Pinky's dad accepts Pinky for who he is. For example, Pinky's dad is okay with his favorite color being pink. Also, he listens to his son's problems and tries to help him come up with solutions, like reminding Pinky that he used to be called Billy.

LINK

Add on to the anchor chart and remind students of the importance of using the strategies outlined on it.

"Writers, you found a lot of details to prove each opinion just now! I've added this strategy to our chart so that you can remember to do it always!"

"As you write, remember that it isn't enough to just say your opinion. You have to back it up! One way to do this is by rereading, looking for evidence, and then adding that evidence to your letter. Don't forget to refer to the chart to help make sure that your letters are convincing! You have so many strategies that you can use now!"

Listening in during the active engagement is a quick and efficient way to find children who need a little extra support. If you find children who are not quite "getting it," you may decide to ask them to stay on the rug after the minilesson. This way the rest of the class can go off to write, and your small group can hang back for the additional support they need.

FIG. 9–1

Using the Classroom Environment to Teach

WHEN I HAD JUST BEGUN TEACHING, I remember spending evenings debating which color markers I should use for this chart or that. What will my Helpful Linking Words chart look like? How will I decorate my door? While making classrooms beautiful and inviting is a lovely thing to do, what you really need to consider is whether or not your classroom environment is *helping you teach*, and more importantly, *helping children learn*. Of course, your charts are working hard to remind children of your teaching, but are children actually referencing them? If done well, the organizational systems you create can support students' independence and sense of repertoire. It is always a happy occasion when children use the supports we supply to work stronger and with more autonomy.

MID-WORKSHOP TEACHING **Helpful Linking Words**

"Writers, can I have your eyes up here for a moment. I want to give you a tip that will help you with your writing. Lots of times when writers are supporting opinions with reasons and examples, there are some words that help the reader. Two of the most important phrases, which we practiced already, are *because* and *for example*. Two other helpful words are *also* and *another*.

"Listen for those words: *because*, *for example*, *also*, *another*. 'Mercy Watson is a special pig *because* she is treated like a person. *For example*, she lives in a house with Mr. and Mrs. Watson. *Also*, she has her own bed. The bed has an *M* on it for Mercy. *Another* reason Mercy is a special pig is because she is so brave. *For example*, she climbs out of her bed in the dark even though she is scared.

"Take a look at your own writing right now, writers. If you've given more than one reason, try using the words *also* or *another* to alert your reader to the second reason. Go ahead, look at your work with your partner!"

After a moment, I said, "Now, if you've given examples, use *for example* and *also*, to make sure your reader catches your examples. Go ahead, look with your partner and see if you can add these phrases!

"Writers, whenever you are using more than one reason or example, these linking words let your reader know you are saying something important. I'll make sure we have them on a chart so you can look for them when you need them." I pointed to a new chart.

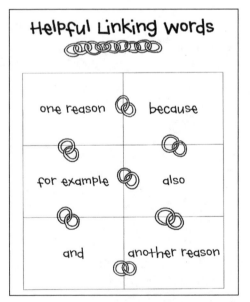

My interest was peaked the second I caught a glimpse of Calder, who had stood up and walked over to the Wall of Fame, where some of our published letters hung. He walked directly to Eliza's letter, lifted his hand, and pointed to each word as he read the letter. Then, as I stood watching, he read it again. Finally, he walked back to his table with a newfound purpose and got straight to work. I couldn't help myself. I had to find out what he had done!

"Calder, what are you working on?" I asked as I pulled up next to him. I gestured for the other children at his table to listen in, knowing that what Calder just did could be something they all might try.

Calder looked up with a start. "Oh, I am writing a letter to my cousin Mizel."

"Oh, wow! Tell us a little about what you are doing to make this letter really interesting for him."

"Well, my cousin is bigger than me, and I really want to write to him because he always gets my mom to let me do big kid stuff, like see PG-13 movies and read *Harry Potter* and other stuff like that."

"So what are you doing to make your letter just right for him?" I nudged him, hoping to find out more about his sense of audience.

"Oh, yeah, well I'm making questions in my letter, like Eliza did. That way the letter will sound cool like hers does."

Satisfied, I complimented Calder in front of the group, naming his strategy so that it was replicable for them all. "Wow, Calder. That is some really important work you did. You know that writers can get writing ideas from other writers, and you chose to take an idea from one of the writers in our class. You studied what Eliza did and then tried the same in your writing. Nicely done!"

Before I left, I reiterated the teaching for Calder's tablemates. "Writers, do you think that you could try what Calder did? Next time you are looking for a new way to make your writing stronger, study a mentor. Look at that mentor's piece, and ask yourself 'What did this writer do to make his writing interesting?' Then try the same in your letter."

Dear Reader,

Mr Watson and Mrs Watson have a pig named Mercy. Mercy loves hot buttered toast and loves extra helpings. Mercy is an unusual pig because . . . you know how pigs don't eat buttered toast and Mercy loves it! Mercy gets to sleep in a bed but pigs don't sleep in bed right? They don't get to drive cars? They don't get to even ride in cars.

Eliza

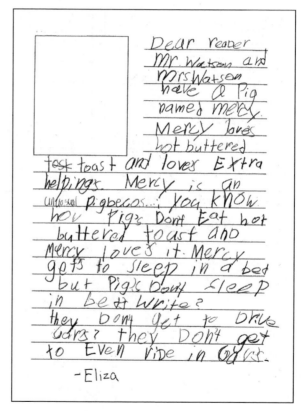

FIG. 9–2 Eliza serves as a mentor for Calder by inspiring him to ask questions.

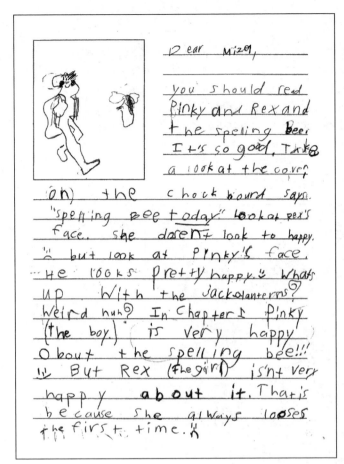

Dear Miza,

you should read
Pinky and Rex and
the spelling bee.
It's so good. Take
a look at the cover.
on) the chock bourd says.
"speling bee today" look at Rex's
face. she dorent look to happy.
"" but look at Pinky's face.
He looks pretty happy." Whats
up with the Jack olanterns?
Weird huh? In chapter 1 Pinky
(the boy.) "is very happy
about the spelling bee!!!
"!! But Rex (the girl) isn't very
happy about it. That is
because she always looses
the first time."

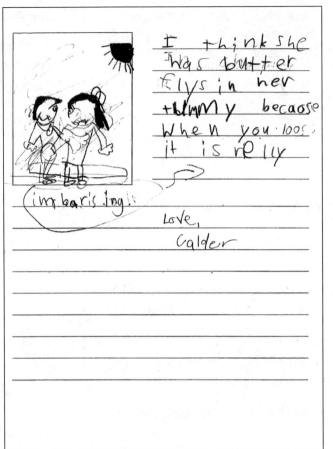

I think she
was butter
flys in her
tummy becaose
when you loos
it is relly

im baris ing!!

Love,
Calder

FIG. 9–3 Inspired by Eliza's letter on the Wall of Fame, Calder asks questions to make his writing more interesting.

Uncovering Life Lessons

Introduce children to the notion of a lesson and ask them to think about lessons they learn from the shared touchstone text.

"Writers, I was talking to Lily earlier, and she was saying that *Pinky and Rex and the Bully* teaches her a lot about bullying and how bad it is. Suddenly, I had an idea! What if kids also wrote about lessons their books taught?

"As readers, we pay attention to character and details and plot and evidence, but it's also important to take time to stop and ask, 'What lessons am I learning from this book? What lesson does this book teach?' Oftentimes you'll find that a book teaches more than one lesson.

"Let's give this a try with *Pinky and Rex and the Bully*. I'll retell a bit of what happens in the story, and you ask yourself, 'What lesson does this book teach?' Are you ready?" The children nodded and I began.

"Okay, let's see," I turned to the first page of the book as I began my retell. "In the beginning, Kevin knocks Pinky off his bike and calls him a sissy. Pinky tries to defend himself by saying that he is not a sissy, but Kevin is just too mean." I turned to the next part of the book, trying to cover a large swath of text with my retell. "Pinky had lemonade and cookies with Mrs. Morgan and Rex, but he was worried and thinking the whole time. The next day, Kevin called Pinky a sissy and a girl, again. Pinky started to get very unsure of himself, and he decided that maybe he shouldn't like pink anymore. He also decided it might not be a good idea to have Rex, a girl, as a best friend."

I stopped there, looking up at the children. "What lessons is this book teaching us so far? What are we learning? Turn and talk to your partner."

After a couple of minutes I reconvened the class, listing on chart paper some of the lessons they'd come up with.

Lessons from Pinky and Rex

- Bullies can be mean.
- It's embarrassing when a bully attacks you.
- Bullies can make you unsure of yourself.
- You should be able to like any color you want.

A share can be a great way to share student thinking in addition to student writing. Here I do not show the class Lily's writing, but instead I share her thinking work.

Usher the children to try the same work in their independent books.

"These would be great ideas to write about in a letter. I bet this would work in your books, too. For just a moment now, will you think about a lesson in one of your books?" I put my finger on my temple to show that I wanted children to think. I gave them a moment and then channeled them to share. "When you've got an idea, turn and talk to your partner."

After listening in for a few moments, I reconvened the children and I shared a few examples I had heard. "Dante is writing about a bunch of mysteries. He noticed that one lesson in *Cam Jansen* is that if you lose something, you should retrace your steps. That seems like an important lesson for mysteries. Eliza is writing about Henry and Mudge. She said one of the lessons in that book is that a pet can make things fun and not scary. Then she thought about it for a minute and said, 'That's true in all the Henry and Mudge books!' Eliza found a lesson that is true in more than one book!

"So remember, writers: whenever you are looking to develop new opinions about the book you are writing about, you can ask yourself, 'What lesson does this book teach?' Then, write a section of your letter about that. I'm going to add this new strategy to our chart."

In this share, I move children from inference to interpretation, pushing them to not only develop ideas about a text but to uncover life lessons.

FIG. 9–4

Why Is the Author Using a Capital Here?

ONE WAY TO TALK ABOUT grammar, punctuation, and spelling is to talk about rules. A friend of ours, who is a linguist, gets very upset by this. One day, while we were walking through the Museum of Modern Art together, he explained that claiming that there are rules in language is like claiming that there are rules for painting. He said, "There are conventions, not rules. Rules make language sound rigid and unchanging. Anything that is human cannot be rigid and unchanging, and language is definitely human." As our conversation continued, he explained to me what he meant by conventions, not rules. Conventions are the way most people typically use punctuation, spelling, and grammar. Rules, on the other hand, are the way you *must* use these things.

Our friend (who, like any great linguist, is rather verbose) went on to point out that the beauty of language is that people create *with it*, the way they would with a brush and some paint. Punctuation and grammar have the ability to affect the mood, tone, and message of a piece of writing. As he was talking we passed a Picasso painting. "Picasso went against the standard conventions and created cubism, thus creating a new convention. That convention influenced the art world forever. Writers do that, too," he concluded. "They can break with the conventions of language and use conventions unconventionally, and they often do this to spectacular effect."

We have never forgotten this conversation, because it helps us to think differently about how we talk about and teach conventions in the classroom. In this session, we will encourage you to teach your children how to use capital letters conventionally, but we will do it by having the children study an author's use of capitals, rather than learn rules. We will use the inquiry method that we have used throughout the year to teach craft, thus channeling children not only to think about *where* it is conventional to use capital letters, but also *how* and *why*. We hope children will leave this lesson understanding a bit more about the conventions of capitalization, as well as the ways it supports an author's particular purpose.

IN THIS SESSION, you will teach children that authors can turn to mentor texts whenever they have a question about writing. In this case, they'll inquire into how and why an author uses capital letters.

GETTING READY

✔ Clipboards, with a copy of a section of a familiar text or a teacher-created writing sample for students to examine for the inquiry, as well as an enlarged copy for students to see (see Guided Inquiry)

✔ Highlighters (see Guided Inquiry)

✔ Chart paper with the heading "We Use Capitals in Our Writing for . . ." ready to be filled in (see Guided Inquiry)

✔ An excerpt from *Mercy Watson to the Rescue,* or another text, that highlights the use of capitals to create excitement (see Mid-Workshop Teaching)

Why Is the Author Using a Capital Here?

CONNECTION

Let writers know that as their writing becomes more complex, so too does their use of capitals.

"I've been noticing something—you probably have, too—in the books we're reading. The authors use a lot of capitals. And it's a good thing! Like in *Nate the Great*, I love the way *Great* is capitalized, so it's like Nate's whole name. He's not just Nate, the good detective, or Nate, who can be great." I kept my voice low and monotonous as I said these phrases, then revved up for the next words.

"No . . . he is *Nate* the *Great*! Capital *N* for *Nate*, Capital *G* for *Great*!" The children giggled.

"Writers, when you notice a writer using capitals, it's always worth studying what they are doing. It might give you ideas for *what* to write about. Like maybe I'll write a letter about all the ways Nate is *Great*. And it will also give you ideas about how *you* might use capitals. We can start by looking at a letter, and see the capitals there. Then maybe you'll look at your books, too."

TEACHING AND ACTIVE ENGAGEMENT

Name a question that will guide the class inquiry. In this case, "Why is the author using a capital letter here?"

"Today, let's look for all the different ways authors use capitals. We'll ask the question, 'Why is the author using a capital here?' Answering that question should give us new ideas as writers."

Before the session begins, you'll want to set out clipboards and highlighters for each partnership to use during the lesson. For now, ask the children to leave the materials aside and sit down, ready for learning. It often helps to ask children to sit on their materials if they can't resist the urge to play with them!

GUIDED INQUIRY

Set writers up to read a part of a letter about a book, letting them know that they should listen and read along, thinking about the inquiry question.

"Writers, to help us study our inquiry question, I've written a letter about Chapter 1 from *Stink and the Incredibly Super-Galactic Jawbreaker*. I used capital letters in a lot of different ways in this letter, so let's put on our detective hats and study all the different places where we see these capitals. Ready to use your detective magnifying glass? There are copies of my letter on your clipboard, as well as up here on the easel." I put my pretend magnifying glass up to my eye, flipped to the enlarged copy of the writing sample, and repeated the inquiry question aloud. "When we notice a capital letter, let's stop and ask, 'Why is the writer using a capital here?'"

> Dear Reader,
>
> <u>Stink and the Incredibly Super-Galactic Jawbreaker</u> is a very funny book. Stink and his sister Judy are always fighting. In one part, they are in a candy store and Stink says that he is going to tell their dad that Judy is acting like a kid in a candy story. Judy says, "But I AM a kid in a candy store." Then, Stink starts to talk about how the name of the candy store is spelled wrong, because it is named Kandy Kompany, and everyone knows that the words candy and company are spelled with a 'c.' Stink and Judy are both so silly!

The children laughed as I read my letter. "Writers, in a minute I will read this again, so we can be sure that we noticed all the capitals, but for now can you just tell your partner where you noticed capitals and maybe even give your partner a few reasons why you think the author used a capital?" The children turned to tell each other about the capitals they noticed, and I reminded them to also name a few reasons why the author may have used capital letters.

After a moment, I called the children back. "Okay, so we already know a few reasons why this author used capitals. They are the same reasons we use capitals. Let's start a quick chart with the reason we already know."

I titled the chart **We Use Capitals in Our Writing for . .**

As the children called out the tried and true conventions for capitalization that they already knew, I jotted them on the chart (see next page).

Any letter or text excerpt will work for this portion of the minilesson. The important thing is that the excerpt you create has a few varied uses for capital letters. Include many examples. Ideally, one or two of these will already be familiar to children, while the other ones will be new uses the children discover during the inquiry.

You may already have a chart like this in your class. If this is the case, feel free to pull it out and use this session as a time to add to what children already know.

Read through the mentor text a second time, reminding children of the guiding question and pushing them toward closer examination.

"Writers, now let's read through the section again. This time, can you be super careful, like a detective, and notice each and every capital letter the author used? Use your highlighter to highlight the places where you see capital letters. Don't forget to talk about the question: 'Why is the author using a capital letter here?'"

As the children did this, I watched.

Pull the students back together and challenge them to think about the different uses of capitals across the writing. Remind them of the inquiry question and get them working to answer it with a partner.

"Wow! This letter sure has a lot of capitals in only a few sentences! Let's look at the letter carefully now. Think with your partner about our inquiry question, 'Why is the author using a capital here?'

As the children worked, I listened in. This time I pushed children to think deeper about each capital letter. Sometimes I asked, "Are you sure? How do you know?" Or I asked, "Is that the only reason to use a capital there?" I also pushed children to think about what the job of the capital was in each of these instances.

"The name of the store is capitalized. Not the whole word, but the *K* and *K* for Kandy Kompany."

Add the children's observations to the class chart.

Once the children shared their thoughts with a partner, I called them back together and added their thinking to our chart. As we added to the chart, we also chatted about why each of these would be a meaningful place for a capital.

> ### We Use Capitals in Our Writing for . . .
>
> - The beginning of a sentence
> - The first letter in a person's name
> - The first letter in all the words in the title of a place or business
> - All the letters in a word to show that the word is loud or important

"Okay, writers, we can keep adding to our chart as we work today. You may find that when you are rereading your book or writing on your own that you see—or use—another unusual capital. If you and your partner notice something else that you think should be added to the chart, will you write it on a Post-it and put it on our chart? Then we can discuss all of the ways that authors use capitals during our share."

I choose to usher children through two separate readings of the text. I know that the first time through they will notice uses for capitals that they already know about—when beginning sentences, for instance, or for the first letter of a person's name. By listing these known uses and then asking children to read again, I hope to push them toward noticing more unfamiliar instances of capitalization.

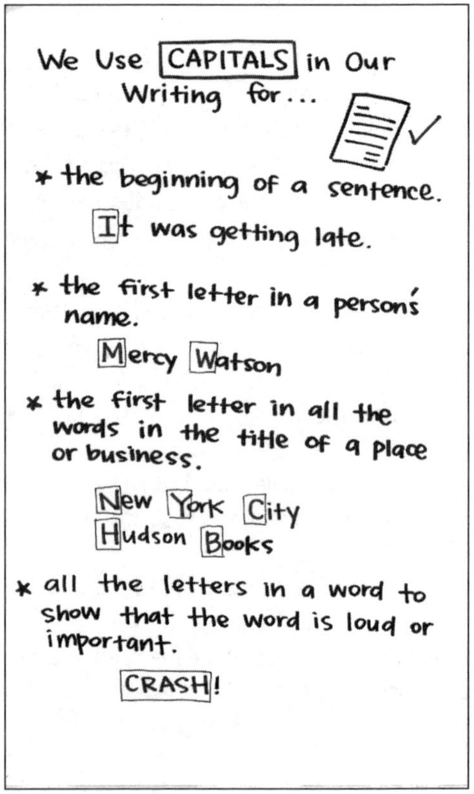

We Use CAPITALS in Our Writing for . . .

* the beginning of a sentence.
  It was getting late.

* the first letter in a person's name.
  Mercy Watson

* the first letter in all the words in the title of a place or business.
  New York City
  Hudson Books

* all the letters in a word to show that the word is loud or important.
  CRASH!

FIG. 10–1

LINK

Send students off to revise, edit, and work on their letters, keeping in mind all the strategies they have learned so far.

"So, writers, are you ready to try this out with your own pieces? As you go off today, I know you'll want to reread some of your writing and think about the detective work we did. If you wrote the title of your book in your writing but you did not capitalize all of the important words, you can go back and change that. Those capitals will make it easy for your readers to know that you are including an exact title. You can also think about capitals as you write more, putting capitals in all the right places right from the start. Remember, you can start by rereading your writing and looking up at the chart to fix up the letters you have already written. Then as you write more, keep your eye on this chart so you use capitals right from the start. And finally, if you are reading and you notice another place authors use capitals, come on up and add it to our chart with a Post-it. Off you go!"

Encouraging children to continue our inquiry as they read their books promotes close reading and the habit of noticing an author's choices as you read.

Combing Our Books for More Fun Conventions

THE WORK OF THIS MINILESSON WAS about ways to use capitals, but it was also about reading as writers and developing the habit of mind to study an author's choices. This could be an interesting day to pull a group of children who are particularly adept at using conventions well and nudge them to think more deeply about conventions and the ways they might be used.

I pulled up to Levi and Sarah. Sarah was busy rereading her *Frankly Frannie* book, and Levi was writing a letter about a *Sonic* comic book that he had brought in from home. I chatted with Sarah about her work for a minute, noticing and complimenting her ambitious plan for adding more to her writing, and then asked both children to work together for a minute.

MID-WORKSHOP TEACHING   **Breaking the Rules and Getting Away with It**

"Writers, can I have your eyes please? As I said in our lesson today, many of you have been noticing ways that authors use conventions in your books. And you know what I keep hearing? Kids keep saying, 'Hey! I didn't know you could do that?!'" The kids laughed in agreement.

"I think what you are noticing is that authors often do things with capitals and punctuation and even spelling that you thought were big fat no-no's, and I want to let you in on a little secret." I lowered my voice for effect. "Authors can be clever and creative with capitals and punctuation as long as they have a reason." There were questioning sounds all around the room. "Yup, its true," I continued. "If an author wants to use lots of capitals, she can. If she wants to write a one-word sentence, she can. The thing is that when authors do something creative like that, they don't just do it. They do it for a reason. That means that when the reader reads the writing, the writing has to sound better and be more meaningful because of the clever stuff the author tries.

"Let's take a look at a few places where authors make creative decisions. Let's start with an example from *Marcy Watson to the Rescue*, here on page 14." I opened the book to the page I wanted to share with the class and held it up for students to see. I had masked the page, so that only the text I wanted children to focus on was visible. I read the words out loud, but in a monotone.

She moved to the end of the bed.

BOOM!

CRACK!

"Kate DiCamillo wrote her words in all capital letters, and she put one word on a whole line. What do you think? Did she do something different? Did she have a reason? Why do you think she did it?" The children chatted and then we discussed how Kate's word placement added emphasis to her words. "It makes you know that what is happening is really bad and awful and loud," Sebastian offered. "Yeah, she definitely had a reason to write it that way, and it told us something very important," said Rimari. "She was telling us, 'This is really bad!'" said Sarah. "We could explain that in a letter."

"Writers, you might actually decide to write *about* how your author uses capitals. Like maybe one of our opinions is that Kate DiCamillo is clever in how she makes some words all capitals. So you can use what you've learned in your writing, and you can also write *about* capitals in your letter."

"One writerly challenge is looking for new ways to use punctuation. Writers often play with their writing a bit, trying out new ways to punctuate, and even new ways to write words and letters. Sarah, I can see that AJ Stern, the author of *Frankly Frannie*, has done some interesting stuff with the way her words look and the punctuation she uses. Can Levi and I study the book with you?"

Sarah and Levi noticed that AJ Stern made up words like *run-aroundy*, using a hyphen to connect the two parts of the invented word. They noted that she often wrote a few words in handwriting font, which they wondered about, but said that was something they saw in lots of the series books they read—especially *Geronimo Stilton*. They said the different fonts made that page more interesting and fun to read.

As we continued on with our mini-inquiry, I did what I often do in a partner conference: encouraged the children to talk to each other, not me. In fact, I positioned myself slightly behind the children as they sat side by side. In this seating arrangement, it was more difficult for them to address me than each other. I coached their conversation occasionally, as I had during the minilesson, saying things like "Why else might the author do that?" or "What does that make you, as the reader, do or think, or know?" This light touch was all they needed to have a thoughtful conversation about conventions.

One convention they talked about was the use of quotation marks around a particular set of words, though they couldn't quite decide what they did. The text read:

Mrs. P. always announces "simply magnificent news" on Thursdays.

At first Sarah and Levi thought the quotes showed that the teacher was talking. Then they decided that she wasn't really talking, but that those were the exact words she would use when she said it. Finally, Levi said, "It could be the name of a thing in their classroom. Like maybe they have Simply Magnificent News on Thursdays, like we have Dance Party on Fridays."

"But if it was the name, why didn't she capitalize it like a title?" asked Sarah.

"Well, maybe it is because the book is supposed to be written by Frankly Frannie and she is just a kid, so it is not right. You know, like Junie B. Jones says things the wrong way all the time!"

Before I left, I encouraged the pair to look at Levi's *Sonic* book, and the discovery there was like a revelation. "Hey! This whole book is capitals. I can't believe I never noticed

it, but I think all comic books are all capitals!" After some thinking, Levi and Sarah had a few theories about this too. "Comic authors do it to look cool." And "They do it because they handwrite the whole book and it is easier." And "Maybe it is because comics don't have as many words, so every word is really important." Finally, Levi and Sarah decided to ask other kids about it at recess. A conventions conversation at recess? My work was done!

An excerpt from Levi's letter before his and Sarah's inquiry:

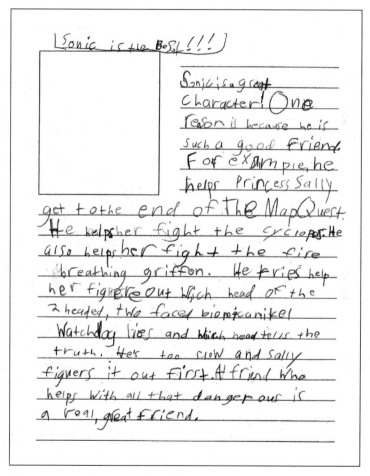

FIG. 10–2 An excerpt from Levi's letter before his and Sarah's inquiry about conventions

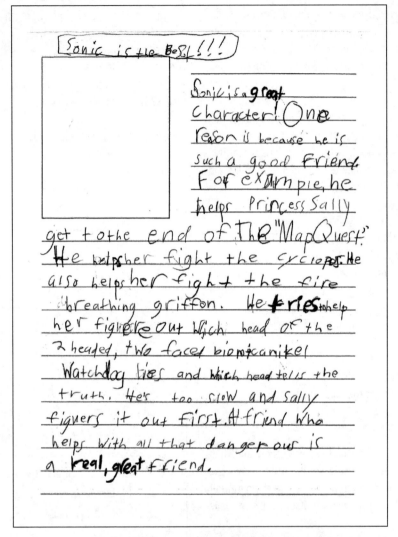

Sonic is the Best!!!

Sonic is a **great** character! **One** reason is because he is such a good **Friend**. For example, he helps Princess Sally get to the end of the "MapQuest." He helps her fight the cyclops. He also helps her fight the fire breathing griffon. He **tries** to help her figure out Which head of the 2 headed, two faced biomecanikel Watchdog lies and which head tells the truth. He's too slow and Sally figuers it out First. A friend who helps with all that dangerous is a **real, great** friend.

FIG. 10–3   Levi revises, incorporating some of what he learned during the inquiry—in this case, he tries using BOLD writing as well as accurate capitals.

Getting Creative with Conventions

Ask several students to share examples of their writing where they played with conventions. Allow the class to discuss whether the writers were effective with their choices.

"Writers, join me on the rug, and if you had some fun with conventions, bring your writing to the rug so the class can help you think about whether or not it works."

The children gathered, and I quickly glanced through the parts that children wanted to share. I chose a few and then set the children up to help each other. "Writers, we are going to see a few examples of kids who are being clever with conventions. Let's take a look and give them a chance to convince us that they can be clever with capitals." First I put up Zac's writing. It read:

It was so funny when Ricky Ricotta gave his aunt a REALLY slobbery kiss. She was grossed out too.

I read the passage out loud and then gave Zac a moment to say why he thought the extra capitals added to his meaning. "I put them there to make you know it was *a lot* slobbery, not just a little. Like in the picture there was slime all over her from the kiss." The children discussed this, and most agreed that the capitals did add meaning. "I say it works!" said Lily.

"I agree," I confirmed. "You can make creative choices about capitals, or any other convention, as long as you do it for a reason—and it works in your writing."

It was so funny when Ricky Ricotta
gave his aunt a REALLY slobbery kiss.
She was grossed out too.

FIG. 10–4

Publishing Our Opinions for All to Read

IN THIS SESSION, you'll teach students that writers often add fun little extras to fancy up their writing and draw in and entertain their readers.

GETTING READY

✔ A small stack of familiar books with interesting features, for example, a map of the setting on the inside cover, a particularly funny "about the author" page, a book with page numbers embedded in small pictures of something important to the text, etc. (see Connection, Teaching, and Mid-Workshop Teaching)

✔ Chart paper with the heading "Extra, Extra—Read All About It! Extras Writers Can Add" (see Teaching and Active Engagement)

✔ The books that students have been writing letters about. Each child should bring a few (see Active Engagement)

✔ Copies of the editing section of the checklist and any other editing tools you've used before (see Link)

✔ Stationery or index cards and markers, so children can write "compliment cards" to each other (see Share)

THIS SESSION WILL BE the second time your students publish in this unit. There are many advantages to publishing repeatedly in one unit. First of all, children write more. Second, they carry forward what they learn with increased independence. Publishing repeatedly gives children many opportunities to move all the way through the writing process; it gives the unit a sense of urgency—an "I better keep going because I'll be publishing in a few days!" energy; and it encourages children to write more pieces, each time applying all that they have learned before and then some. An added bonus of having students publish again and again in one unit is that it gives teachers a chance to try many different "finish up lessons." For the last finish-up lesson, we suggested that children do revisions and edits based on charts and checklists. For celebrating Bend II, we are suggesting something different. We are suggesting writers be creative in how they draw in their readers. Many of the authors your children are studying include creative attention grabbers—your children can also make these choices as writers.

Of course, you'll also want to have on hand the editing tools children have used up to this point. As they make their letters engaging, encourage them to use the "juicy word wall" to develop their vocabulary and spelling. Remind them that checklists are on hand for them to set their own editing goals. Act as if your children know how to help each other and they probably will!

Publishing Our Opinions for All to Read

CONNECTION

Drumroll the upcoming writing celebration. Remind students that writers fancy up their writing before publishing, and ask them to recall which tools located in the classroom they can use as resources to do this.

"Writers, we have a lot of good, hard work ahead of us today, so join me in the meeting area with a few of the books you have been writing about." The children hurried to the rug, and I could feel their excitement for writing. I smiled, proud that hard work had officially become "fun." "Today will be our last day writing letters about books." Before I could finish my sentences the children let out an audible sigh of disappointment. "Don't worry," I added. "Next week we will still be writing our opinions about books, but it will be different, and I'm keeping that work a secret until later.

Hinting at "secrets" keeps writing time fun and exciting, while peaking the children's interest.

"Today we will polish and publish the writing we wish to share. Remember that when writers are almost ready to share their writing with the world, they ask, 'What can I do to make this the absolute best it can be?'" As I said this, many children pointed to the checklist posted on the wall. "Aha! It is true! You have been using your checklists to help you make your writing even better. What else?" The children pointed in every direction, reaching their fingers toward the charts, the word wall, and the Wall of Fame that held many letters from last week's celebration. "That is also true. You can use the tools in our classroom to help you make your writing the absolute best. Anything else?"

This time there was a pause, and I made a show of staring at the kids, each in turn, almost pointing with my eyes. Finally, Sarah burst out with, "Our classmates!"

"Yes, yes, yes. Your checklists and tools and classmates can all help you to make your writing its absolute best, and that will be the first part of your work today, finishing up the plans you have already made. But there is one more thing I've been meaning to share with you." I trailed off again for effect, wanting the kids to take on yet another challenge. "When you want to publish, you often want to add a little something extra. You know authors often add something to make their writing unique and fun. Take a look at this book." I held up *Geronimo Stilton*—a class favorite. "Do you see how Geronimo made his book have all of these funny letters in different shapes and sizes? Or what about this one?" I held up *Stink* to show off the page at the end of each chapter that featured a small comic. "Or this one?" I held up *Mercy Watson* and pointed to a few pages where little pictures of toast were used to embellish the page numbers and to decorate the author's name. The children laughed as I shared all the quirky little extras in these books. There were murmurs, too. "I never noticed that!" some said, while others declared, "I saw that before!"

The "extras" you'll point out in this lesson are so very second grade, as they are abundant in books written for this age. Make sure to choose examples that show up in your class's favorite books.

Writers, today as we get ready to share and send out into the world our newest letters about books, let's fancy them up with the same kind of fun extras that our favorite authors use." Everyone cheered.

"Great! Let's conduct a quick study to inspire us. Let's take a few minutes to figure out a bunch of ways to add fun and extra meaning to our letters, by looking at what our favorite authors do."

❖ Name the teaching point.

"Today, I want to teach you that writers often add fun little extras to draw in and entertain the reader. They can study published books and ask themselves, 'What did this author do to make this story more interesting and fun?' And then they try the same things in their letters."

TEACHING

Start a quick study of one of the books you have written about.

"Writers, let's start our study with *Mercy Watson to the Rescue*. I'm going to look through this book and try to find quirky and fun extras that Kate—the author—and Chris—the illustrator—included to entertain us or help add meaning to the story."

Think out loud about what you see, noting not just the feature but why you think the author or illustrator included it.

I displayed the book and began to think aloud. "Hmm, the cover has a great picture of Mercy running and the Watsons stuck upstairs in their bedroom. Great picture, but I wouldn't call that an extra. I'll keep going." I turned the page to the title page and paused. "Nice page, but nothing really extra here." I turned the page again, and now the dedication page was revealed. "Oh! This is a dedication page, and look, here is a little something extra. There is a little decoration next to the dedication. It's a piece of toast on Mercy's plate, right next to the dedication. Hmm, I wonder why Kate and Chris put that there?" The children started answering, and I included their comments as I continued. "Well, Mrs. Watson always shows her love for Mercy with buttered toast, so maybe Kate and Chris thought adding the toast here would let us know how important toast is to Mercy!"

Start a quick chart to list different extras writers might include.

"Writers, let's start a quick chart. Let's make a list of all the extras we notice in our favorite books, and while we do let's think about why we think the authors and illustrators included them."

You'll notice that I up the ante here, not just noticing quirky details but seeking to understand why an author or illustrator has included them. I do not expect that all children will understand, in this one short lesson, that the extras in a text often add meaning, as well as fun. But there is no harm in offering the opportunity to do so!

I flipped to the piece of chart paper where I had already written the heading:

"Extras Writers Can Add"

Then, I added the first bullet to our list.

- Decorations that share a fun detail from the book

"Let's study some more." We continued to study *Mercy Watson to the Rescue*. This time I let the children help me, calling out and quickly discussing why Kate and Chris might have included each extra.

Soon our list also included:

- Big words that take up a lot of the page
- Pictures of the covers of all the books in the series

"Writers, we already have three extras from just one book, as well as some ideas about why the author added them in!"

ACTIVE ENGAGEMENT

Invite your students to find the extras in their books, asking why the author may have chosen to include them.

"Writers, you all have your books with you. Let's open up this study and take a look at all of these books. Partner 2, will you pick up one of your books? Look carefully for the extras the author and illustrators include. And Partner 1, it will be your job to make sure you are both thinking about why the extra is there. Go ahead and give it a try!"

Before long the room was filled with children's voices. I asked the children to share not only *what* they noticed, but *why* they thought that particular extra was included.

Sebastian began. "*Geronimo Stilton* has lots of words that are made out of cheese." He giggled. "I think it's because Geronimo is *so* into cheese. He loves it." We added the following bullet to our list.

- Words written in fancy fonts or fonts that match what they mean

Elias added on. "We noticed something kind of the same but a little different in *Frankly Frannie*. In this one part (he held up the page for all to see), the numbers that say what chapter it is are made out of things like tape and Sharpie markers." Elias stopped, so I prompted him to add on. "Elias," I said, "why do you think the illustrator made the chapter number out of office supplies?"

Without a moment's hesitation, Elias added on. "Frannie *really, really* wants an office job."

A few more children shared what they had found, and soon we had added the following bullets.

- Words written in fancy fonts or fonts that match what they mean
- Words and letters made out of pictures
- Chapter titles that are jokes
- Maps that go with the story
- Pictures that go across pages

"Wow! Writers, our authors and illustrators sure do have fun adding lots of entertaining extras to their books. I bet you are already starting to imagine what you'll add to your letter when you get back to your desk."

LINK

Remind the children of their ongoing work and invite them to add the work of including extras to their plans for the day.

"Writers, I can tell you have some fun ideas about extras you might put in your letters to make them more fun!

"As you go off to polish and publish, I know you want your letters to be fabulous. Here are some other tools you might want." I pointed to the checklists on their tables. "How many of you feel like you could use the editing portion of the checklist on your own?" Many thumbs up. "Excellent." I pointed to the Juicy Word Wall. "How many of you feel you could use the word wall to improve your word choices and spelling?" More thumbs up. "Okay, off you go then! I can't wait to see your fun and fabulous letters!"

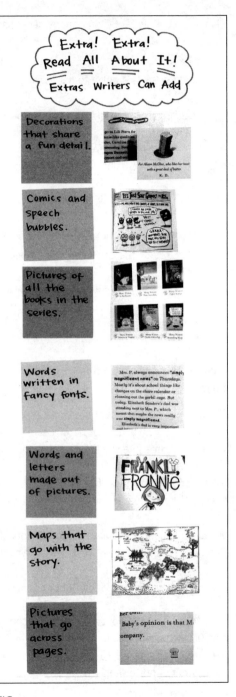

FIG. 11–1

When Is Handwriting a Priority?

Y OU MIGHT CHOOSE TO MAKE TODAY THE DAY that you spend a little time on handwriting. We typically do not recommend having a whole class of second-graders copy over their writing to publish. There are a number of reasons for this, but the first and most important reason is that it is just so time-consuming. Recopying a piece of writing that is three or four or five pages long would take most second-graders one or two whole writing periods. When you consider that it took children about that much time to write the piece in the first place, the pay off just isn't there. If you have children recopy, that is time taken away from making more writing. Another reason is that children at this age often make lots of mistakes when they recopy, and the job can become very upsetting. Finally, *many* children will simply write less to begin with if they know they will need to recopy in the end.

All of this being said, there are times when recopying makes sense—in moderation. One case is if you have a child who still has trouble forming certain letters—*b* and *d*, let's say. You might try having a conference with that child, asking her to go back though her writing to check and, when necessary, rewrite those letters. This can be a helpful task.

Another time for recopying might be when a group of students have a page or so where there have been so many great revisions that the page is hard to read. In this case, you might call together the group and give the children a fresh piece of paper—or two—and encourage them to recopy so that the reader can follow all of the fabulous elaboration they included.

Finally, you might have a child or two type a piece of writing that they are particularly proud of and that they are willing to work on typing outside of writing workshop time.

MID-WORKSHOP TEACHING
Extras Can Add Extra Meaning

"Writers, can I have your eyes up here for a moment? Adam did something very clever in his letter. He was writing a letter about how clever Nate the Great is to figure out all these clues. And in the margins of his letter, he put pictures of the clues, in order! So as you read the letter, you also *see* some of the clues! Isn't that clever? Adam really thought about how his extras would not just be fun, they would actually be important. You might do that work, too—add extra *meaning* as well as fun."

Some teachers allow typing during writing time. In these cases, teachers allow for just a few children per publishing period to work on classroom computers during writing time.

If you feel that you have children who would benefit from these supports, remember that when you make the choice to have children work on handwriting, you are also making the choice to stop them from doing other revision and editing work. Therefore, it is often helpful to decide that the children who work on handwriting during one publishing period will not dedicate time to it for the next.

Publishing for an Audience

Settle children in the meeting area, sitting them next to a child who is not their usual writing partner. Give a small, celebratory speech.

"Writers, let's share some of our writing! Take one last look at your work and make sure it is just right, then join me on the rug." As the children came to the meeting area I put them in new partnerships, and gave them stationery cards and pens. "Let's share with new partners today so we get to hear more of each other's writing.

"Writers, today we celebrate." With these opening words I gave a little commencement-type speech, telling the story of their journey so far and highlighting some of the especially sophisticated and momentous work I had witnessed."

Ask children to turn to their partners and begin sharing, using the stationery you handed out to write compliments to each other.

When my story of our journey came to a close, I said, "So, writers, now it is time to share our letters. Please look over your letters and find a part that you think is especially fantastic. Find a part that shows off your very best work. When you've found that part, show me with a thumbs up."

I waited until children were ready, giving them a few moments to make their decisions. "Writers, now you will get a chance to share in your groups. Each of you will get a chance to read a portion of your letter. Readers, don't forget to tell your listener how you will share your writing with the world. Will it go in a book basket? Will it get sent out to someone special? Will it go on our Wall of Fame? When you are listening to your partner, you have a job too. I know you will be so impressed with your friends' work and that you will want to write compliments on the cards that you are holding. Get started!" I moved from partnership to partnership quickly, so that I could hear a bit of most children's writing. Children laughed at the extras and exclaimed at the information, but best of all, so many children said, "I have to read that book!"

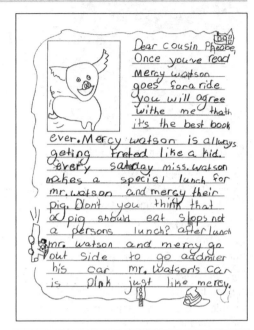

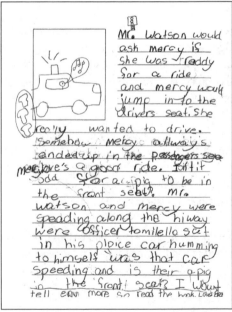

FIG. 11–2 Bea's published piece is written to a favorite cousin.

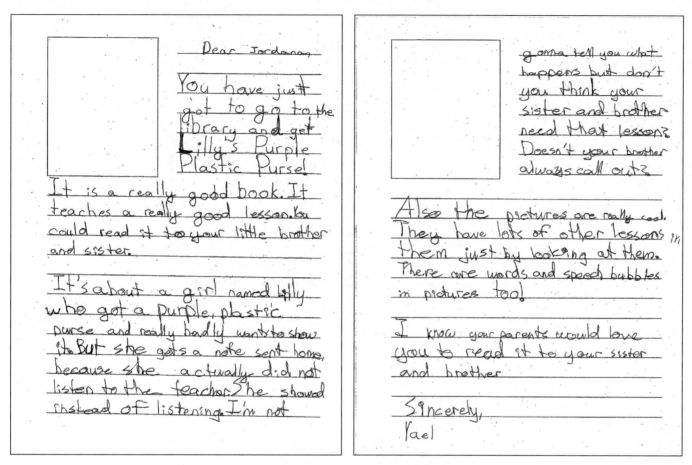

Dear Jordana,

You have just got to go to the library and get Lilly's Purple Plastic Purse!

It is a really good book. It teaches a really good lesson. You could read it to your little brother and sister.

It's about a girl named Lilly who got a purple, plastic purse and really badly wants to show it. But she gets a note sent home, because she actually did not listen to the teacher. She showed instead of listening. I'm not

gonna tell you what happens but don't you think your sister and brother need that lesson? Doesn't your brother always call out?

Also the pictures are really cool. They have lots of other lessons in them just by looking at them. There are words and speech bubbles in pictures too!

I know your parents would love you to read it to your sister and brother

Sincerely,
Yael

FIG. 11–3   Yael's published letter reflects her love for a favorite classroom picture book.

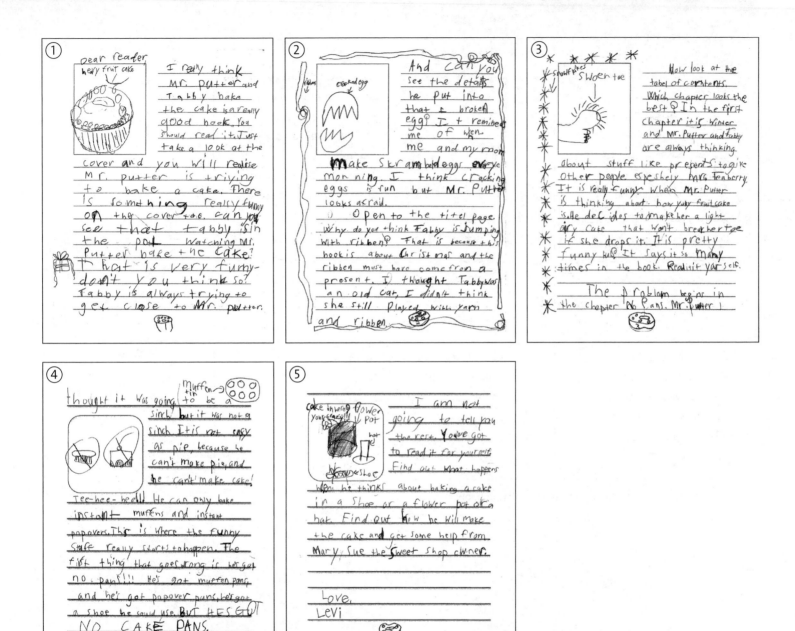

1) Dear reader

heavy fruit cake

I really think Mr. Putter and Tabby bake the cake is a really good book. You should read it. Just take a look at the cover and you will realise Mr. putter is trying to bake a cake. There is something really funny on the cover too. can you see that tabby 'sin the pot watching Mr. Putter bake the cake? That is very funny- don't you think so? Tabby is always trying to get close to Mr. putter.

2) cracked egg

And can you see the details he put into that I broken egg? I t remined me of when me and my mom make skrambold eggs every monning. I think cracking eggs is fun but Mr. Putter looks afraid.
   Open to the titel page. Why do you think Tabby is Jumping with ribben? That is because this book is about Christmas and the ribben must have come from a present. I thought Tabby was an old cat, I didn't think she still played with yarn and ribben.

3) snowflakes   swoen toe

Now look at the tabel of contents. Which chapter looks the best? In the first chapter it is winter and Mr. Putter and tabby are always thinking about stuff like presents to give other people espeshely Mrs. Teaberry. It is really funny when Mr. Putter is thinking about how yuky fruit cake is. He decides to make her a light airy cake that won't break her toe if she drops it. It is pretty funny Because It says it so many times in the book. Read it yourself.

   The problem begins in the chapter No Pans. Mr. Putter I

4) muffen tin to be a

thought it was going to be a sinch but it was not a sinch. It is not easy as pie, because he can't make pie, and he can't make cake! Tee-hee-hee!!! He can only bake instant muffens and instant popovers. This is where the funny stuff really starts to happen. The fist thing that goes wrong is her got no pans!!! He's got muffen pans, and he's got popover pans, he's got a shoe he could use. BUT HE'S GOT NO CAKE PANS.

5) cake in her oven flower pot
your crazy!!!
hat
horseshoe

I am not going to tell you the rest. You've got to read it for yourself. Find out what happens when he thinks about baking a cake in a shoe or a flower pot or a hat. Find out how he will make the cake and get some help from Mary Sue the Sweet shop owner.

Love,
Levi

FIG. 11–4   Levi's published piece: a letter he chose to revisit and add to from Bend I. Notice the pages he added in this new revision as well as the extras.

Writing Nominations and Awarding Favorite Books   BEND III

And the Nominees Are . . .

IN THIS SESSION, you'll teach students that writers of nominations choose topics that they have strong opinions about, making cases for them by including evidence.

GETTING READY

✔ Four books that you are interested in possibly using as nominees (see Teaching)

✔ The books that students have been writing about throughout the unit and possibly some new favorites (see Active Engagement)

✔ Nomination paper (lined paper with a place for a heading or award description) (see Link). Stock your writing center with this paper as well.

✔ "Make It Stronger, Longer, and More Convincing" chart (see Conferring and Small-Group Work)

✔ An award nomination mentor text, enlarged for students to see (see Share)

AS YOU BEGIN THE FINAL PORTION OF THIS UNIT, you will ask children to change gears a bit. Your students have been busy at work writing about the strong opinions they have about the books they read. Across the next bend, you'll invite children to nominate their most cherished books for awards. Tell them to gather up their very best and most treasured choices, because awards are seriously hard to win. Tell them to choose thoughtfully, because while children will continue to write their opinions about books in these nominations, this time they will be writing to judges—judges who choose the winners for book awards. For some children, the mention of judges will call to mind the very serious faces of the Supreme Court, while others will immediately picture the more entertaining faces of those who make decisions on television competitions. You'll want to decide if you will have real judges, perhaps a committee of a few children, parents, or teachers, so children can write to a specific audience. Either way, the children will likely understand how important it is to impress and persuade an audience of judges and bring that sense of importance to writing this week.

By this time in the unit, your students are already doing some very sophisticated work. You've taught them to state an opinion, to support it with reasons and details from the text, and use linking words to connect those reason and details—adding details from the text is third-grade work according to most state standards! So what more is there to teach? We believe that if the children can do all this, then they can surely do even more. In the coming days, we will suggest that you teach students to use quotes to supply further text evidence, make comparisons between texts and collections of books, add introductions and conclusions, and lastly, teach one another all that they know!

To kick off all of this, you might rally student energy around this new and exciting prospect of writing to judges, making the case that their favorite books deserve awards. You will say, "If you want to convince a judge, you can't just do one of the great things we tried when writing to friends. You must do *all* of them!" Across this final bend, you'll remind students to draw from their growing repertoire of strategies to write in increasingly more structured and persuasive ways.

And the Nominees Are . . .

CONNECTION

Tell students a story about visiting a bookstore and noticing all of the award-winning books. Explain that this is the work they will be undertaking: writing nominations for their own favorite books.

Students gathered in the meeting area with their favorite books in hand. I asked the children to either place these nominees beside them on the rug or to sit right on top of them in their spot. Once everyone had settled in, I began with a story. "Yesterday afternoon, I went to the bookstore to buy a new book for my nephew. His fourth birthday is coming up, and I wanted to find a wonderful book for him since he loves to read. When I asked the shop owner for some recommendations, she guided me toward a display and said, 'These picture books have won the Caldecott Medal for having some of the very best illustrations.' Then, she pointed to a table with stacks of chapter books. 'And these books,' she explained, 'have won the Newbery Medal. These books tell some of the very best stories about some of the most interesting characters.' There was even a shelf of nonfiction books that had won the Orbis Pictus Award. The bookstore owner said, 'These are some of the very best books, so I'm sure you'll find something your nephew will love.'"

I shifted from my story to address the students, leaning in to continue. "Judges had to decide which books should get these awards. These awards let readers know just how special these books are. Being in the middle of that bookstore, surrounded by these award-winning books made me think about you and the work you've been doing, writing letters about the books and characters *you* think are the very best. I bet you'd want to give these books your own awards if you could!" The children smiled brightly in agreement.

"Well then, let's do that! Let's write nominations for the books *we* love the most, explaining why they deserve awards, too." The children clapped their hands and sat up in their spots, excited about the new venture.

❖ **Name the teaching point.**

"Today, I want to teach you that writers of nominations choose topics that they have strong opinions about. They then ask themselves, 'What do judges need to know about this nominee to understand why it deserves an award?' They make their cases and support their opinion with reasons and details."

Again I start with a story to draw my students in and to provide some schema for those who may not know very much about book awards.

You'll want to define a term like nominations *for your students, but you need not stop the rest of your teaching to dryly read out a definition. Here I tuck in the meaning as I continue to build excitement for our new undertaking.*

TEACHING

Walk students through the steps you take: first choosing a book to nominate, then thinking aloud about what makes your chosen book so special and the reasons why it is deserving of an award.

"Watch how I think carefully about each of my nominees to decide which book I feel most strongly about to plan and write my first nomination." I placed my four selections on the ledge of the easel. "I have grown to love each of these books, and I know you have as well. *Mercy Watson* makes me laugh out loud. *Pinky and Rex* teaches me important lessons about friendship. *Nate the Great* keeps me guessing. *Knuffle Bunny* has such unique illustrations." I paused, tapping my chin to make my thinking visible. "But which of these books do I feel the most strongly about? Which book do I think readers absolutely need to get their hands on?" I left some quiet space to consider this question, allowing students to think alongside me. Then, I tapped my finger on *Pinky and Rex and the Bully*. "You know, even though these other books are such a joy to read, I think of all these stories, *Pinky and Rex* is the most important book for readers to know about." I looked up at the students. "Now watch as I think about a nomination to explain why this book deserves an award.

"What do judges need to know about this book to understand why it deserves an award?" I asked myself. "Let me think about the most important reasons and details I need to include in my nomination to convince the judges." I picked up the copy of the book, studying the cover illustration and quickly scanning through several pages. "Well, one *huge* reason I think *Pinky and Rex and the Bully* is a book people absolutely need to read is the important lessons this story teaches readers, like how you should be true to yourself no matter what others might say. Another important reason," I continued, rehearsing my writing aloud, "is that the characters you meet in this story are so interesting and real. Pinky and Rex face problems and experience emotions that many of us know about, like dealing with bullies, or feeling embarrassed or confused."

Debrief.

I shifted my attention back to the students. "Did you see what I did to plan the nomination I'll write first? I looked across my selections to decide which of these nominees I feel *most* strongly about. Then, I asked myself, 'What do judges need to know about this book to understand why it deserves an award?' so I could plan my writing out loud, giving the most important reasons and details to support my opinion."

ACTIVE ENGAGEMENT

Give students an opportunity to practice, first by choosing a book to nominate, and then by planning the reasons why their book deserves an award.

"Now you try it! Take out the nominees you've selected and think carefully about each book to decide which one you feel *most* strongly about—the book you think people shouldn't go one more day without reading." I gave the students a moment to reflect on their books. I voiced over, "Tap your finger on the book you'll nominate first to show me you're ready to start planning." I scanned the rug until each child had made a decision.

Here I am dramatizing the process of choosing a book to nominate. This is because we want children to really consider their topic choice. As students weigh their choices, they begin to develop the thinking that will become their nominations.

If your children were part of a writing workshop in first grade, they will know well the job and the process of a judge—this was part of the persuasive unit in first grade. If you think that your students are less familiar with judges, however, you might add to this lesson, saying a few words about how judges make decisions.

Notice that we not only expect that children will choose their topic today, but that they will plan and write their first nominations, too.

"What do judges need to know about this book to understand why it deserves an award?" I paused, pushing writers to rehearse their nominations. "Just as you looked at every detail to uncover your opinions to write letters," I reminded, gesturing toward the "Uncovering Our Opinions about Books" chart, "plan what you'll say to judges to convince them to award the book you're nominating. Use your fingers to list the reasons why you think the book is one of the very best. In a moment, you'll turn and share with a partner." I moved in to coach students individually as they planned aloud.

Quick reminders about what children already know often help them get started.

I knelt beside Grace as she flipped through the pages of *Amelia Bedelia and the Baby*. "Grace, why do you think this book should receive an award? What makes it so great?" "It's really silly," Grace replied succinctly. "Because . . . ," I continued. "Because Amelia Bedelia is always doing the wrong thing. She never understands what she's supposed to do. It makes me laugh!"

Don't be afraid to push the level of children's thinking with lean prompts. The active engagement provides a perfect opportunity to support students as they try new, difficult work.

"Can you find a part in this story that shows an example of that?" I nudged. Grace skimmed through the pages, pausing at an illustration of Amelia Bedelia holding a can and a cardboard box. "She was supposed to give the baby a bottle, but she thought the baby would break it so she gave the baby a can and a box, instead. She was supposed to feed the baby!" Grace giggled.

I echoed Grace to frame her claim in an organized way. "So one important reason *Amelia Bedelia and the Baby* is a book readers need to know about is that it is a very silly story, because Amelia Bedelia is always doing the wrong thing, instead of what she is supposed to do. For example, she gives the baby a can and a box, instead of giving the baby a bottle to feed her." Grace nodded. "Keep going! What else should judges know? What else makes this story special?" I moved on to quickly check in with another student.

Restating a child's idea in a more organized way models for children how to take their thought and make it clear before writing.

Ask students to rehearse their writing with their partners.

Soon after, I prompted partners to rehearse together. "Now, pretend that your partner is the judge to whom you are writing. Practice what you'll include in your nomination to tell the judge all the reasons and details that prove why the book you've chosen deserves an award. Partner 1 will begin. Partner 2 will be the judge."

LINK

Send students off to write, reiterating the procedure you introduced during the minilesson.

After reconvening the group, I restated the strategy to propel their ongoing work across the bend. "So, writers, remember, whenever you are writing nominations, it is important to choose the books you feel most strongly about. Then, make sure to support your opinions with important reasons and details. One way to do this is to ask yourself, 'What do judges need to know about this book to understand why it deserves an award?' Then include those details in your writing.

"I can already tell that you are ready to get started! I've stocked our writing center with special paper that you can use to record your nominations. Let's begin!"

Many times we use the link to reinforce the day's minilesson, as well as remind students of other strategies that they have learned along the way. Today's link is a bit different, however, since it is the beginning of a new bend. The work they will be undertaking for the rest of the unit builds on the work of the first two bends. But it is important to rally energy around the award nominations, so we choose instead to focus solely on today's teaching as we send students off to get started.

Getting Mileage Out of Any Learning Tools You Have at Hand

TODAY YOU MIGHT take a quick look around. Who is off and running—maybe ahead of the rest of the class—with this new kind of writing? Who is just putting along? For both kinds of writers, one of the most supportive things you can do is help them to see how the minilessons across the whole unit can do more for them.

With your off-and-running writers, turn their attention back to charts and any learning tools you have at hand—little checklists, demonstration texts, anything that can help them uncover strategies that they haven't slowed down enough to try. For the putting-along writers, you might help them take the teaching of past minilessons in a more bit-by-bit manner. In either case, you might find that pulling a chart—or any kind of learning tool—close to your writer and studying it might be just what he or she needs.

Consider the conference I had with Morgan. While Morgan was very excited to write about *The Banana Split from Outer Space*, he was staring at his paper after only a few minutes of writing.

"How's your nomination coming along? What are you working on today?" I asked, trying to put a little pep in my voice to pep up his somber face. I looked down at his paper (see Figure 12–1) and read:

> It should get the freeze your bones award. The Banana Split from Outer Space, it is so cold there's ice-cream all through the book.

"I got this part. I think I wrote it funny," Morgan stated.

"Hmm." I didn't say anything more, waiting to give him the chance to elaborate.

"Yeah, 'cause I gave it a funny award name, see!" As he spoke he pointed to the words "freeze your bones award." Then he paused. I remained quiet, waiting for him to continue. "But now I don't know what to write." He looked down at his paper. "I'm stuck."

MID-WORKSHOP TEACHING
Using Reading Post-its to Write More

"Writers, can I have your eyes please?" I stood near one table, holding a student's book that had Post-its sticking out from various pages. "Writers, I want to give you a quick tip. You already know that one way writers get ideas for writing about books is to look for places in their books where they had ideas to share. In our class, we often use Post-it notes to mark parts of our books that we want to discuss with our partners." The children agreed. "Well, you can look across *all* of your Post-its to find the ones that show off your fanciest thinking—the Post-its that really show off the most important ideas you have as readers. Then, you can use those Post-its to help you write about your books, using those parts to support your opinion.

"Everyone, take a moment right now and look through your book." I paused while children looked through their books, voicing over, "Maybe you have a Post-it marking an important scene. You can write about that! Maybe you have a Post-it marking something surprising the character did. You could write about that! Maybe you have a Post-it marking a part that made you wonder. You can write about that, too!

"Put a thumb up once you've found your fanciest Post-it." Once I saw that children were ready for the next step, I continued, "Now, think about your Post-it. What else can you say to talk more about that part?" I gave children a moment to compose their thoughts. "Find a good spot to add that thinking to your nomination."

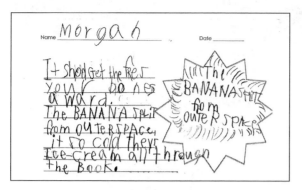

FIG. 12–1   Morgan's nomination before conference

Again I paused for a moment. I could just give him a strategy, but we were more than halfway through second grade, and it had become a habit for Morgan to wait for help. I decided to ask a question that might make Morgan realize he knew how to help himself. "How did you know to write what you have now? Where did this idea come from?"

"Well, you told us to write for an award, so I wrote the award the book could get."

"Hmm. So, what next?"

Morgan turned back to his paper. Then he looked up at me. I didn't say anything, so he looked back down at the paper. "Well, I wrote that there is ice cream all through the book." Again Morgan paused. I had a feeling that if I just waited a little longer Morgan would talk himself through the process. "I could tell where the ice cream is in the book." Morgan stopped again. Even when he looked at me, I continued to peer at his paper. "I could do a retell to show where the ice cream is, 'cause maybe the judges don't know, if they haven't read this book."

Finally, I smiled and said, "Morgan, you know how to do this. You knew how to start. You knew how to give your opinion, and you just made a plan for how to show it. Keep going. And if you get stuck again, you can do what you just did. You can talk about what you have done so far and then push yourself to find the next step. And if *that* doesn't work, use some of the charts we've made." Morgan peered up at me and smiled a bit. "Look around, do you see a chart that can help?"

"I like that one." Morgan pointed at the "Make It Stronger, Longer, and More Convincing" chart.

"Can that chart help you?"

"Umm, I could back up my opinion by looking for more places with ice cream and prove it."

"You sure can, Morgan!" Before I walked away I named the steps Morgan took to get "unstuck" and finally added, "Morgan, you are getting to be a very grown-up writer, using opinions and retelling and evidence from your book. Just remember that grown-up writers also work hard to get unstuck all by themselves."

> It should get the freeze your bones award. The Banana Split from Outer Space–its so cold there's ice cream all through the book. Stanley sells ice cream. He's the main character in the book. Did you know how on Mars they eat ice cream? Well that's what it says in the book. Zelmo sells ice cream on Mars. There's only 3 flavors fleenzil, uplaloo and plinkee. Zelmo might be able to help Stanley. Zelmo said "I came to earth to find new flavors for the Mars ice cream fair."

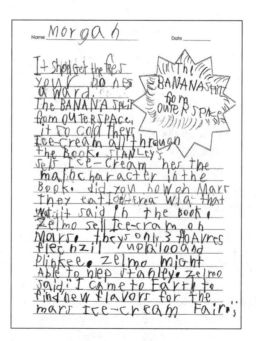

FIG. 12–2   Morgan's nomination after conference in which he finds inspiration from a familiar chart.

A Mentor Text Inquiry

Guide students to study a mentor text to explore what the writer has done, think about what they could transfer to their own writing, and make decisions about ways to elaborate further.

After the children gathered in the meeting area, I began. "You already know that writers learn from other writers, that they read and think to themselves, 'What did this writer do that I could try, too?' Just like you've begun writing nominations for the books you believe deserve awards, writers in the world nominate the books they think are some of the very best. I want to share with you an announcement written for a chapter book that won the Theodor Seuss Geisel Award. The book is called *Tales for Very Picky Eaters*. Let's study this and think, 'What did this writer do that I could try in my writing?'"

I had rewritten the piece on chart paper so that students could follow along as I read aloud.

> "Tales for Very Picky Eaters, *written and illustrated by Josh Schneider, published by Clarion Books, an imprint of Houghton Mifflin Harcourt Publishing Company.*
>
> *Each of the five chapters in 'Tales for Very Picky Eaters' recounts James' refusal to eat yet another disgusting, smelly, repulsive, lumpy or slimy food. Not only picky eaters, but all readers will delight in the outrageous suggestions along with the off the wall rationale from his very clever dad for why he should become more adventurous in his food selections. James turns the table on his father when he decides to become more daring and bold in his meal choices and actually tries something new.*
>
> *Schneider captures the attitude of the picky eater. The illustrations have a cartoon-flavor and are executed in watercolor, pen and ink, and colored pencil.*
>
> *The dialogue presents some preposterous situations but even the most challenging words are presented in context so beginning readers can easily discern their meaning. The touches of humor make this book an engaging page turner," said Geisel Award Committee Chair Carole D. Fiore.*

"What do you notice? What did this writer do to convince others that this book deserves the award?" Some hands shot up. I gave children another moment to compose their thoughts before prompting partners to discuss their observations. "Will you turn and share three things this writer did that you might try?"

I moved across the meeting area, listening in to partnerships. Dante told his partner, Rimari, "He retells a little bit about the story so you know what it's about."

"Yeah, but he doesn't give the whole story away. He just tells a little bit," Rimari added.

I moved on to another partnership. "There are details about the pictures and how the illustrator used all kinds of art supplies to make them, like watercolor and pen and colored pencils," Bea observed.

"And look at the last part. It's a quote from someone talking about the book. There are quotation marks around it," Christopher noted, pointing up toward the chart.

I reconvened the group and asked partners to share their observations, naming them back using concise and transferable language. I jotted these strategies on sticky notes, posting them beside specific examples in the text.

I summed up the class's work by reminding children that they could continue to look back at this mentor to spark ideas for elaboration, adding more to their own nominations.

Prove It! Adding Quotes to Support Opinions

IN THIS SESSION, you'll teach students that opinion writers use specific evidence from the book to support their thinking. Sometimes the portion of the text that proves their opinion can be added directly to their writing through the use of quotation marks.

GETTING READY

✔ "Make It Stronger, Longer, and More Convincing" chart (see Teaching)

✔ Your own nomination writing about the touchstone text (see Teaching)

✔ *Pinky and Rex and the Bully* by James Howe or other touchstone text (see Teaching)

✔ Revision strips and tape (see Teaching)

✔ Students' nomination writing as well as the books they are writing about (see Active Engagement)

✔ Post-it notes (see Active Engagement)

✔ "Using a Quote?" chart (see Mid-Workshop Teaching)

✔ Nomination paper (see Share)

ERE AT THE Teachers College Reading and Writing Project, we debated back and forth about whether or not second-graders should be taught to use quotation marks when citing evidence from a book. Most state standards do not call for this work for a few more years, and the children can write beautiful opinion pieces without quoting the text directly. However, many second-graders feel perfectly comfortable with the use of quotation marks when including dialogue in their stories; in fact many of them have been using quotation marks in their narratives since first grade! For these writers, the transition to quoting texts can feel quite easy.

We're also interested in getting kids to elaborate and write more than we are in anything else, and using quotation marks can be an elaboration strategy. But then again, we worried that children might just start copying pages and pages out of their books, forgetting entirely about the nominations they are writing in the first place. You can see that we deliberated about this for some time.

Ultimately, we decided to go ahead and teach children that writers use quotation marks to quote the exact words found in a text, just like when you quote someone speaking in a story. Then, we watched what happened. The good news is that the children we taught this to loved it and, frankly, didn't seem to think it was too much of a challenge. They were already using their books to copy the title and the author information, so using the book to add what a character said made complete sense! In fact, many children even started to quote *other* parts of their books so successfully that we had to teach them some ways to introduce those quotes.

In the end, you'll want to assess your writers before following the suggestion for today's teaching. Take a moment to look across students' writing folders and your own conferring notes to determine if students are, on the whole, ready to take on this next endeavor. If you find that many use quotation marks for dialogue in their stories, go for it! Keep that tone of "Isn't this grand?" going, and your students will likely rise to the challenge as you rally the troops for above-grade-level work.

Prove It! Adding Quotes to Support Opinions

CONNECTION

Share your observations about the impressive work students have been doing in this unit.

Students quickly gathered in the meeting area with their most recent nomination and the corresponding book. Once they had placed their materials beside them in their spots, I began.

"Boys and girls, you have been impressing me with the work you have been doing in this unit. Yesterday we began writing nominations. Most of you are on your second piece. Some of you have even begun a third piece! You have been working so hard as readers and writers and thinkers to make your nominations better than anything you've ever written before! I've even watched you stop to jot ideas down in reading workshop and use them during writing workshop to add evidence to your pieces, just like you did as letter writers! I'm so impressed!"

Then, I leaned in as if to whisper the juiciest of all secrets. "You know, I was thinking about all this amazing work that you're doing in second grade this year and I was *so* proud that I *actually* started to brag about you to one of the first-grade teachers!"

Recall prior learning about quotation marks and hint at the new work they can do.

"And I have to say, he was pretty proud to hear about it, too. As we were talking, he told me that *last* year, in first grade, you wrote reviews! Thumbs up if you remember doing that." Thumbs shot up in affirmation. "Well, do you know what else I learned about the work you did as review writers that impressed me even more? I learned that sometimes you would include what other people had to say about your topic, like experts about the topic or people who had been to that same place or seen that same movie. You would add quotes to make those people talk right inside your review, even using quotation marks like you do when you write stories.

"Writers, you know that when you want to persuade someone, it helps to quote what other people have to say about the topic—just like you did last year. But writers use quotes in other ways, too. In fact, when writers write about books, they often quote a part of the book to support their opinion."

Students won't know how much writing you expect them to make unless you tell them. Here I mention how many pieces children are making partly as a celebration and partly so children can self-assess by comparing how much writing they are making.

If you have any student pieces from the prior year on hand, or the teacher's demonstration piece, now would be a good time to show these. Artifacts can help to remind students of prior skills.

Notice how I make the connection to last year's work, but then raise the level of that work by teaching another way to quote.

❖ Name the teaching point.

"Today, I want to remind you that opinion writers sometimes use specific evidence, exact words from the book to support their thinking. You can reread your texts to find a part that proves what you hope to show. Then, you can use quotation marks to add those exact words to your writing." Before moving on, I added an additional bullet to an already familiar process chart from earlier in the unit, revising students' growing repertoire to extend what they already know as opinion writers.

Make It Stronger, Longer, and More Convincing

- Introduce the book.
- Write your opinion.
- Give reasons using BECAUSE.
- Give evidence from the book—use FOR EXAMPLE.
- Talk to your audience.
- Add sections or pages to your letter.
- Use juicy story words.
- Back it up! Use evidence from the book to prove your opinion.
- Use quotation marks " " around exact words.

TEACHING

Demonstrate how you use direct quotes from the touchstone text to support your opinion. Reread your writing, thinking about your opinion. Then, go back to the text to find evidence to support your opinion. Finally, add in the direct quote, using revision strips and quotation marks.

"Writers, right now I want to show you how I can use exact words from *Pinky and Rex and the Bully* to help prove the ideas I have about this book and make my nomination even more convincing." I picked up my demonstration piece, rereading it aloud quickly.

"Now, let me stop and think to myself, 'What do I want readers to know about Pinky? What do *I* think about him?'" I left a moment of space to contemplate this, making the steps of my process more explicit for students.

"Well, I think Pinky is the kind of boy who cares about being a good friend, even when others try to tease him. I think Pinky is brave because he stands up for what he thinks is right." Then, glancing back toward the process chart on the easel, I pointed toward the second step. "Now, I'll need to find a part of the book that proves it." I picked up my copy of the book and began to skim the pages, thinking aloud, "I remember the part when Pinky stands up to Kevin. I can

FIG. 13–1

We often use and touch the chart as we demonstrate—showing children just how we expect they will do this same work.

use the pictures to help me find that scene, or I can use the table of contents to find it. Here it is! On page 36." I read a short excerpt aloud.

> *Pinky walked straight up to Kevin and poked him in the chest. "It's none of your business what I like,"*
> *he said. "Or who I play with. I'm not a sissy and I'm not a girl. And if you think so, it just shows how*
> *dumb you are." Kevin's mouth hung open as Pinky poked him a second time and then walked away.*
> *"Come on, Rex," he said, "let's go."*

"I can zoom in on this scene to choose the exact words I can use in my nomination to prove that Pinky is brave. I think that I could add these two sentences at the beginning. I'll add it to a revision strip with quotation marks around it and the page number so that my reader can find the exact part I am talking about." I did this quickly and placed the revision strip accordingly.

> For example, on page 36 in the story, "Pinky walked straight up to Kevin and poked him in the
> chest. 'It's none of your business what I like,' he said. 'Or who I play with.'"

Restate the entire teaching point, recapping your process, to reinforce the demonstration.

"Writers, did you see how I stopped to think about what I want readers to know about the book? Then, I looked for places where a quote could give an example straight from the book. Finally, I added this quote to my writing with quotation marks."

ACTIVE ENGAGEMENT

Give students an opportunity to plan for their independent work. Ask students to reread their writing and make a plan for how to make it stronger by quoting the books they are writing about.

"I bet you're itching to give this a try in your own nominations. Well, right now, let's plan for the quotes that you might add to your writing to support your opinions. Reread what you have written so far and ask yourself, 'What do I want readers to know?' Do that now." As children began to read over their pieces, I voiced over to guide their thought process. "Think about the opinions you have about the book. What makes it so special? What ideas do you have about the character? When you have your idea ready, hold onto it, like a firefly." I scanned the meeting area as students cupped their hands together, signaling they were ready to share.

"Now, will you quietly show your partner your idea, telling the opinion you have about your book? Share your thinking with each other quickly." I moved in to listen.

"I loved how Peter H. Reynolds added so many details and a lot of action," Kate whispered to her partner.

"I love Chrysanthemum's name and how she learns that she should love it, too," Eli voiced back.

I don't stop to talk about every little decision I make here. I don't explain the page number, the for example, and so on. If you catch yourself explaining each word you write, remember that the true focus of your demonstration can get lost in all that explanation. Keep your demonstration clean. If you realize children need more, you can always revisit the teaching.

My voiceover helps children through the steps of finding a place to add a quote, before they jump into looking through their books.

I reconvened the group after a short time. "Now, back it up with words from your book! Find a part that proves your idea and think about which exact words you can quote in your writing to help your reader understand your thinking. Then, put a Post-it down on that page to mark the spot."

As students scanned the pages of their books, I sat alongside Eli. "Eli, you told your partner that Chrysanthemum finally learns to love her name. Can you find where in the story that happens?" I gave Eli a moment to flip through a few pages, offering a lean prompt, "Use the pictures in the book to help."

"Right here!" he announced, pointing down at a picture of a cheerful Chrysanthemum.

"Now zoom in to decide which words on the page will help you show your reader that Chrysanthemum loves her name," I nudged.

"She blushed. She beamed. She bloomed," Eli read.

"You can put quotation marks and add those exact words to your writing. Put a Post-it on that page so you can find it easily, later."

I paused the students in their work when I saw that nearly every child had placed a sticky note in their book. "I can tell that many of you have found a part to quote to help prove your thinking about your book. You might even push yourself to find *another* part to quote to prove your thinking even more or to prove *another* idea you have."

LINK

Remind students to call upon all they know to make their writing strong and powerful. Give them an opportunity to get started on their revision work, right in the meeting area, before sending them off to work independently.

"Writers, you are getting so grown-up. You're each becoming the kind of writer who thinks about all the things you already know about making writing longer, stronger, and easier to read! That way, every new piece you write is even stronger than the one before it.

"And from now on, whenever you write about books, you can quote parts of the book to prove your thinking. You can use quotation marks to add the exact words to your writing. If you know what you want to add to your writing, will you give a thumbs up?"

I looked around at the raised thumbs and said, "Get going on your revisions, adding those parts into your nominations, right here on the rug! I'll come around to check in with each of you and send you off when I see that you're ready." I gave the students a few minutes to begin working independently at their rug spots.

The active engagement is always a good time to listen in and take stock of what children are doing. You may decide to look for children who need just a little support to take off with this new work. If you find that a little more coaching is needed, remember you can always invite a few children to stay for a small group after the minilesson.

As children begin working in the meeting area, you can move across, coaching in as needed, signaling children, one at a time, to return to their seats.

How Much Is Too Much? Cutting Our Quotes Down to Size

TEACHING SECOND-GRADERS TO QUOTE A BOOK is much like teaching kindergartners to repeat a word. Anyone who has taught writing workshop in a kindergarten classroom knows what happens the day you teach children that writers use repetition. You send the children off to write, and not more than five minutes into writing time, between four and six children have written something to the effect of "I love my mom so so so so so so so so so so so so so so . . . much." How exciting it is to fill a page with print and, oh, how easy it is to do when you can just repeat the same word over and over and over again. A very similar phenomenon will happen in second grade right after you teach children to use direct quotes from the text. Quoting is such a good way to fill a page, and of course the book that is being quoted is a favorite, by a favorite author, so isn't it satisfying to use a lot of that author's words?

Today, you will likely find that there are a number of children who start to quote their books and then just keep going and going. For these children, a small group is certainly in order. You might choose to start the group by addressing the dilemma straight on. "Writers, there is something very tricky about quoting a book. Quotes really help you show the reader—in this case the judges—how great your book is. You want to quote what the author wrote because it is just so perfect. Maybe the quote goes perfectly with your opinion, or maybe it supports your reason for liking the book, or maybe the way the author wrote it is just lovely. On the other hand, if you use too many of your author's words, your reader can lose track of *your* idea and *your* writing. So we need to quote *just enough*.

"That is the hardest part about using quotes in your writing. Knowing when it's time to *stop* quoting the book and get back to writing about *your own* ideas and opinions. Let's try it together. I am adding on to my nomination about the Pinky and Rex series, and in this part of my writing, I am trying to show that Rex is a really good friend. I found a great spot where adding a quote will really support my idea, and I even found a part in the book to quote. Let's work together to figure out where to stop the quote. Let's read the quote sentence by sentence. At the end of each sentence, we can ask

---

MID-WORKSHOP TEACHING   **Introducing Your Quotes**

"Writers, I see many of you are adding more quotes to your nomination writing, to give your readers an example straight from the book and prove your thinking. Nice work!

"I want to give you a little tip about adding quotes. Just like when you wrote introductions to introduce readers to your information books, your quote needs a little introduction, too, so the reader can understand what it's about and why you included it in your writing.

"Take a look at the different ways you might introduce a quote." I revealed a chart with a few simple prompts to support the use of transitional phrases.

Using a Quote?

First, give it an introduction. Try one of these:

- For example, in the book it says . . .
- On page ___, you can read . . .
- (The author) writes it like this . . .

"I know you want to try this right away, so turn to your partner and plan how it might go. Say it out loud to decide which one fits best." As the children rehearsed these phrases, I listened in and encouraged them to try out different introductions and even to invent their own.

ourselves, "Does this still support my opinion?" When it doesn't back up my opinion anymore, we'll stop the quote. Ready?"

I read my writing out loud as I laid it in front of them. I also had my copy of *Pinky and Rex and the Spelling Bee*, ready to refer to.

> Rex is a great friend to Pinky. She is always giving him good advice. One example is when Pinky is worried that the new kid, Anthony, will beat Pinky at the spelling bee. Pinky is all scared about losing, but Rex gives him good advice.

"Right there, I thought I would quote exactly what the book says—the advice that Rex gives. That would be a good idea right?" The children agreed, so I opened to the page in *Pinky and Rex and the Spelling Bee* to find that part. "Okay, I'm going to read you the part, and at the end of each sentence, let's ask, 'Does this quote support my opinion?'" I began to read.

> *"So what if he does?" said Rex, with a shrug. "You know what you told me: 'It doesn't matter.'"*

I paused. "Does that go with my opinion that Rex gives good advice?" The children nodded vigorously, so I read on.

> *"But everyone will laugh at me. And I won't be the champion speller of the whole second grade anymore."*

I stopped, clearly thinking. "Hmm, does *that* go with my point about Rex? Does that line show that she is a good friend?" The children thought for a minute and talked back and forth. At first they were unsure, stating that it was still about the spelling bee, but finally decided that it was not about Rex giving good advice. We decided to stop the quote after the first sentence.

I did this once more with the children, knowing that this difficult strategy required some additional practice. Finally, the children turned their attention to their own quotes, cutting them down to size.

Before I left them, I reminded them of the whole strategy. "So, writers, we know that we can use quotes to support our opinions. The important thing about quotes is that we also need to know when to stop them. We can figure that out by reading each sentence in the quote and then asking, "Does this still support my idea? If not, cut it!"

Nominate Another! Planning More Pieces

Ask students to brainstorm other books that they think are worthy of awards. Give them an opportunity to get started on their next piece of nomination writing.

Before calling students back to the meeting area for today's share session, I placed a new sheet of nomination paper on each child's spot. Then, I asked the class to bring a pencil with them to the rug. Once everyone had gathered, I began.

"I am so eager to learn more about the books you love *so* much that you want to give them awards. Wow! These must be some of the very best books, huh?" The children smiled.

"Well, I know whenever I'm asked to name my most favorite book, it's a hard question to answer. I have *so* many favorites and I can never name just one. I bet you have that same problem!"

"I do because I love every Elephant and Piggie book. I have almost all of them at my house!" Lexie exclaimed.

"Well, guess what? We don't need to decide on just one favorite book to nominate. We can write lots of nominations for all the books we love! Some of you have already begun to write a second or even a third piece. Right now, think about another book you think should get an award. Maybe it's a different kind of story. Maybe it deserves another kind of award because it's special in a different way." I gave the students a few moments to brainstorm possibilities, but it was easy to tell they were each brimming with ideas.

"Get going on your next nomination. Start planning what reasons you'll give to convince the judges why *this* book deserves an award, too. We'll have a few minutes to work right here. Then, you can put these into your folder to continue working on tomorrow. It's always helpful for writers to have a plan for what they'll write next." I moved across the rug, crouching down to support writers as they began a new piece.

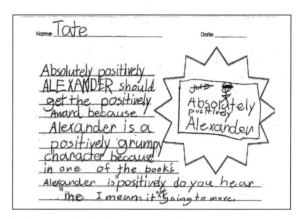

FIG. 13–2 Tate starts a new nomination.

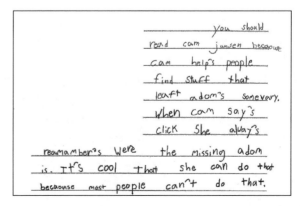

FIG. 13–3 Dante starts a new piece about Cam Jansen.

Good. Better. Best.

IN THIS SESSION, you'll teach students that writers often make comparisons to support their opinions. When writing about books, they compare characters, series, or kinds of books to explain why they think one is better or best.

GETTING READY

✔ A collection of several books that you can compare in your writing. The books can be part of a series or of a similar genre (see Teaching and Active Engagement)

✔ "Uncovering Our Opinions about Books" chart (see Teaching)

✔ Your own nomination writing (see Teaching)

✔ "Exploring the Lay of the Land" chart (see Mid-Workshop Teaching)

ONE WAY TO EXPAND YOUR CHILDREN'S WRITING capacities is to expand what they are writing about. If students have been writing pages about one book, imagine the rise in volume that will result in writing about a series or collection of books. However, there is yet another reason to move to writing about more than one book at a time. It will lead your writers into the high-level analysis work of making comparisons. You'll be supporting your second-graders' ability to tackle evidence-based argument work, along with using text-based evidence. Impressive! It is important to ensure that your writers are really thinking—weighing and comparing, selecting and rejecting.

You'll continue this bend with some comparison work—helping writers think about what's the same across texts. Don't forget that what seems stunningly obvious to us as adults, such as that Jack and Annie appear in every *Magic Tree House* book or that in every story, the tree house spins and travels to a new place and time, may still be fresh realizations for your students. Some students, of course, will be ready to move beyond these literal plot similarities to comparisons about characters, issues, and lessons. Across this session, you'll introduce this range of possibilities.

Keep a careful eye on how this work is going and its impact on volume. If students were writing more while explaining than they are now when they are analyzing, perhaps they need to rehearse their thinking with a partner, or perhaps they should explain *and* analyze for different parts of their nominations. Writers strengthen their understanding of a genre when they write a lot. So remember, while this new work builds on students' repertoire, encourage students to continue the work they have already been doing as nomination and letter writers.

Good. Better. Best.

CONNECTION

◆ COACHING

Tell students a story about watching movies and then comparing them in a discussion with friends. Relate this to the kind of thinking and writing they can do across books.

"Writers, last night, I rented a movie with my friends. We decided to watch *Up*, the Pixar movie about an old man and a young boy who travel far away in a house carried by a thousand balloons." The children's ears quickly perked up at the description of this familiar movie. I paused for a moment, signaling for the class to settle before continuing with my story.

If you have a Smart Board or LCD projector, showing a few short clips of trailers will enliven this connection.

"Well, once the movie ended, my friends and I began talking about *all* the movies we love, and the characters we like the best. We began comparing *Up* to the other animated movies we know and sharing our ideas about which we thought was the best. My best friend insisted the characters in *Finding Nemo* were funnier than the characters in *Up*. But she thinks the characters in *Despicable Me* were the funniest."

Using examples your children are familiar with encourages engagement and helps children better understand the concept you are teaching.

This sparked an immediate debate across the rug, and the class talked, for a moment, about favorite movies and kinds of movies.

"Children, I realized while I was talking with my friends, that we had so much more to say when we started comparing characters and series of movies. And suddenly I thought, '*Wait* a second! We can do this with our nominations! We can write about more than one book and make comparisons!'"

✤ Name the teaching point.

"Today, I want to teach you that nomination writers often make comparisons to support their opinions. When you're writing about books, you can compare characters, series, or kinds of books to explain why you think one is better, or best."

TEACHING

Show students how you compare similar books. Model how you think closely about what aspects of the book you are comparing, and then include this thinking in your writing.

"Writers, it seems to me that the easiest way to write about more than one book at a time is to make comparisons between books that are similar, like in a series or genre. I can think about how *Pinky and Rex and the Bully* is better than other *Pinky and Rex* books. I might even compare *Pinky and Rex* to other books about friendship or other realistic fiction stories. I've gathered some books to make a collection. This way, I can make comparisons to say more and add to my writing."

I placed two other *Pinky and Rex* titles along the ledge of the easel, along with *Ivy and Bean*, another realistic fiction story featuring best friends. I purposefully selected texts that were familiar to the students. "Because these books are similar, I can compare *Pinky and Rex and the Bully* to explain how it is better, or what parts make it the best."

I picked up *Pinky and Rex Go to Camp*. "Let me look back at our 'Uncovering Our Opinions about Books' chart to help me decide what I might think more closely about to compare this book to *Pinky and Rex and the Bully*." I gestured toward the chart, thinking aloud to help students follow my decision-making process.

Notice how, as always, I introduce new thinking work—in this case, comparison—and follow that quickly by reminding children that this will be added to their writing.

Model how to use a familiar chart in a slightly new way. This encourages transference.

Uncovering Our Opinions about Books

Writers can study . . .

- Characters
- Favorite parts
- Pictures
- Titles
- Covers
- Lessons

"Well, the main characters in both books are, of course, the same, but I could think more about my favorite parts of each story to think about why I like *Pinky and Rex and the Bully* more. Let's see . . . My favorite part of *Pinky and Rex Go to Camp* is when Pinky starts acting funny when Rex shows him the letter about camp. That's why you realize he's not excited about going to camp."

I put down the one book and picked up the other. "Now my favorite part of *Pinky and Rex and the Bully* is when Pinky meets the bully. When Pinky first meets the bully it made me feel really nervous, and I wanted to turn the page to find out what would happen next. Wait, I can add that to my nomination to show why this story deserves an award. But instead of just saying it's *better*, let me think of a word that describes *exactly* what I want to say about these two parts." I tapped my chin, thinking aloud to push vocabulary. "Hmm, more interesting? More exciting? I've got it! It's *suspenseful*. That's what makes it better. The scenes in *Pinky and Rex and the Bully* are more *suspenseful* than the scenes in *Pinky and Rex Go to Camp*, especially when Pinky first meets the bully. I didn't know what the bully was going to do next or how Pinky would react. It makes you want to turn the page to find out what will happen next. Let me add that to my nomination." I picked up my demonstration piece to write:

> The scenes in <u>Pinky and Rex and the Bully</u> are more suspenseful than the scenes in <u>Pinky and Rex Go to Camp</u>, especially when Pinky first meets the bully. I didn't know what the bully was going to do next, or how Pinky would react. It makes you want to turn the page to find out what will happen next.

Debrief, reviewing the steps you went through to compare books and think closely about the comparison.

"Did you see how I did that? I thought about other books that are similar to the story I want to nominate. Then, I thought about what parts of the book I might compare to explain how one is better, or the best. And finally I added my comparison into my writing."

ACTIVE ENGAGEMENT

Give students an opportunity to practice this work using books from your collection.

"Will you help me find even more ways to compare *Pinky and Rex and the Bully* to other books in the series or to ones you know? Let's use our chart to uncover more opinions about these books. How else can we show it's better or the best?" I distributed several copies of the texts in my collection, so that each partnership would have two different titles to use for this comparison work. I prompted partners to share their opinions about the books. Some partners picked up their own books as well.

"*Pinky and Rex Go to Camp* and *Pinky and Rex and the Bully* both have a problem, but this one," Noah went on, raising a copy of *Pinky and Rex and the Bully*, "is more serious, and it teaches a bigger lesson than that one." I moved on to listen in to another partnership.

"The pictures in Pinky and Rex are better than the ones in Ivy and Bean books because they are colorful," Stella told her partner, opening up to a page of *Ivy and Bean*.

"Yeah, it looks like the illustrator," Lexie paused, flipping back to the cover. Then, she filled in, "Melissa Sweet. She probably took more time to make the pictures prettier with watercolor."

While this lesson is about comparison, you'll find that it provides a great opportunity to teach about word choice too.

You might decide to have children bring a few books to the meeting area and try this in their own writing during the active engagement. This will help children transfer their new learning right there in the meeting area.

LINK

Remind students how making comparisons between books is another kind of evidence that can support their opinion. Give them an opportunity to come up with some possible books to compare.

"So remember, writers, whenever you write about books, it helps to make comparisons to support your opinion. You can compare characters, series, or kinds of books to explain why you think one is better or best. Let's do this now while it's on our minds. I want everyone to take a minute right now and think about the book that you are currently writing your nomination about. Do you have it in your head?" I paused and waited for students to nod in agreement. "Okay then, now, take a moment and think about which book you might be able to compare it to. Is it part of a series? Are there other books with similar characters? Or a similar genre? Once you have another book in your head, turn and share this information with your partner." I gave students a minute to talk, circulating among the group and helping students who might have needed suggestions for books to compare. "Okay, writers, thumbs up if you're ready to go off and get started on making your nominations even more convincing! Off you go!"

Even this late in the unit, encourage students to make a plan before they leave the rug for how they'll use their writing time. This helps children remember to use new strategies in concert with the ones they have learned before. You'll also send a clear message: writing workshop is a time for productivity and hard work.

Pushing Children to Think Deeply about Books

YOU MAY BE NOTICING that although your children are being thoughtful about their books, they are not necessarily thinking as deeply or analytically as you would like. Perhaps their ideas feel more like facts than opinions. Then too, they may have developed opinions that feel superficial or mismatched to the depth of thinking you believe they are capable of. Take my conference with Sarah, for example.

I sat down alongside Sarah, who was working on her nomination about the book *The Twits* by Roald Dahl. I stopped her just as she was beginning a new sentence. "Sarah, what will you write about next?"

"I want to teach my readers something. I want to teach them how Roald Dahl writes a lot of books about weird and mean and silly people. Lot's of his characters are like that."

I nodded enthusiastically, prompting for more information. "That's so interesting. Tell me more." "Well, I mean I think it is really funny and I burst out laughing all the time," Sarah giggled.

I noted the fact that Sarah was approximating something—namely, teaching her reader something important—but that she was settling for a somewhat obvious fact about Roald Dahl's books.

I began by complimenting Sarah, allowing this compliment to lead directly to my teaching. "Sarah, what I see you trying to do is very impressive. You want to teach your reader something. You want to let them in on a secret about Roald Dahl and his books. When we teach about our books, though, we want to make sure we are teaching others about big, important ideas. One way to do this is by thinking about the lesson a book (or series of books) teaches, and then writing to explain that lesson to your reader. Let me show you what I mean."

I modeled a bit of the work aloud, taking a lesson from Pinky and Rex and writing-in-the-air to show how I'd teach my reader about that lesson. "The *Pinky and Rex* series,"

I began, "teaches kids that it is okay to be themselves. It does this in many ways." I leafed back through the book, looking for evidence as I spoke. "For instance, Pinky has a friend named Rex who always stands by his side and makes him feel okay. He also has parents that don't mind if he plays with dolls or loves pink, even if it's something

MID-WORKSHOP TEACHING
Still Haven't Found What You're Looking For?

"Writers, I am noticing that many of you are moving from book to book to book, trying to make sure that you are adding examples from many of your books. That is just what writers do when they write about collections of books. They look through the books, rereading and finding examples to include! Give yourselves a pat on the back!"

"I am also noticing that some of you are getting lost in your books—you're spending more time reading than writing. I want to give you some quick advice to help you with this. Sometimes, you have an idea about the part you want to talk about, but then it's hard to find it again. Put a thumb up if that has happened to you." Lots of thumbs went up.

"Well, we *already* have something in our room that can help! During reading time, we know that before we even begin reading a book, we can get the lay of the land and preview the parts of the book. How many of you do this as readers?" Hands stretched high as I walked over to our "Exploring the Lay of the Land" chart hanging above the library that we used in reading workshop.

"Let's look over it together to remind us of ways we can find what we are looking for in our books!" We read the chart together. *(continues)*

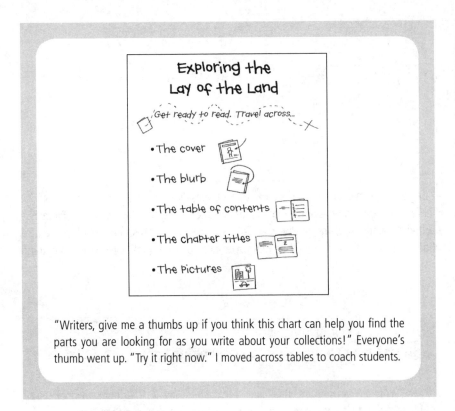

Exploring the
Lay of the Land

Get ready to read. Travel across...

• The cover

• The blurb

• The table of contents

• The chapter titles

• The pictures

"Writers, give me a thumbs up if you think this chart can help you find the parts you are looking for as you write about your collections!" Everyone's thumb went up. "Try it right now." I moved across tables to coach students.

that girls usually do. Also, Pinky gets helped by neighbors and other people who stand up to the bullies and tell him it's okay to be different."

I quickly debriefed the moves I made before asking Sarah, "Do you see what I did there? Instead of teaching my readers something they might have already noticed (like the fact that Pinky likes Pink, or that he and Rex are friends), I pushed myself by explaining a lesson the book teaches. Let's try the same with your book.

"You said that Roald Dahl has lots of mean, cruel characters, right? Let's think together. What might he be trying to teach us by including these characters in his books?"

Sarah and I talked a bit before she realized that things generally end badly for Dahl's mean characters. "I don't think he likes mean characters. Bad things usually happen to them. Maybe he wants us to not be mean like them," she said, "'cause it's bad to be that way and bad things will happen to you."

Praising Sarah, I ushered her to work immediately. Soon she had written several paragraphs on the lessons Roald Dahl teaches (see Figure 14–1).

The twits
by Sarah
Roald Dahl writes about alot of mean rude characters. I think he wants to teach children that being mean and rude is really bad so he makes his mean and rude characters have a bad time. The funny thing is that his mean and rude characters are fun to read about. It is fun to read about the twits because they are so disturbing and disgusting. They hate children and they dont like to clean up after themselves they are crazy dirty people. They do lots of bad things too. they play bad tricks on each other all the time. I think Roald Dahl is teaching us a lesson. He is teaching us not to be rude and snotty. I know he does not want us to be like the twits because he makes them get the Shrinks. That is when thir head shrinks into their neck and

their neck shrinks into and their body shrinks into their feet. then they are gone so Roald Dahl must not like what they did

FIG. 14–1   Sarah works to write about the lesson Roald Dahl teaches in many of his books.

Finding the Just-Right Word

Ask a student to share her writing. Give the class an opportunity to notice the things that the writer did to make her writing convincing.

"Writers, come join me on the rug. Bring along your own writing folders and pencils, too." Once the class had gathered in the meeting area, I pulled Petra close to me. "Class, just as you are all writers and learners, you are also writing *teachers*. You work with partners to help make each other's writing even better!

"Well, Petra has been working extra hard to write about one of the characters in the book she is nominating. She's grown some big ideas about Stink. Let's listen carefully to Petra's nomination (see Figure 14–2) to think about what she's done already that will help to convince the judges." Petra began to read aloud.

> I think Stink is very, very nice. He is especially nice to animals. I know he is nice because he tries to make his hamster and his cat like each other a lot. He tries to get them to like each other by putting them together and making them play together, but it doesn't work because hamsters and cats are kind of like dogs and cats—they just don't get along. He is also nice to animals in book 4 when he helps the pet shop owner Mrs. Birdwistle give away all of the hamsters that have overrun her shop. He doesn't just help her with 8 hamsters, he helps her with all of them! He rides in a van all the way to Virginia Beach to find a new happy home for those hamsters.

"Quick, tell your partner some things Petra did as a writer to be convincing." I gave the class a few moments to share. Then, I named back their observations quickly.

"So, we noticed how Petra made her opinion clear, beginning her piece with exactly what she thinks about the character. But, also, we noticed that she supported her opinion with reasons and also with details from the story. Well done, Petra!" Petra smiled shyly.

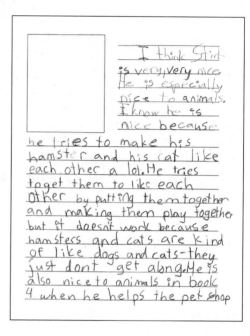

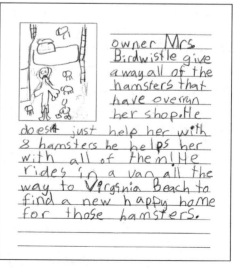

FIG. 14–2   An excerpt from Petra's nomination

Draw students' attention to language in the writing that is somewhat ordinary. Give them an opportunity to brainstorm, coming up with more precise language.

"Petra was telling me she wants to make her nomination even *more* convincing. One way to do this is to find the just-right word to say exactly what you mean. That way, your ideas will be easier for readers to understand. Petra, we can all help with this!" I turned back to Petra's piece, reading aloud the first line.

> I think Stink is very, very nice. He is especially nice to animals.

"Hmm, nice. Nice," I repeated aloud, pondering over the word. "Well, *nice* helps me understand a little bit about Stink, but what other words could Petra use to show Stink's character—what kind of person he is?" I asked the question without eliciting responses right away, giving the students time to mull over possibilities. "He is especially nice to animals," I reread. "That helps us get to know Stink a little more. What might be some just-right words we can use, instead of *nice*?" I signaled for the students to turn and talk.

"*Caring*," Noah offered. "Because he takes care of the animals."

"Yeah, or *loving*," Calder returned.

"Maybe you could write, 'I think Stink is very, very kind,'" Levi shared with his partner, Petra.

"Yeah! He *is* kind. He takes care of all the animals," Petra agreed.

I called the students back to celebrate all the just-right words they had discovered. "Petra, I bet you have so many ideas about how you can revise your nomination to use just-right words that show your reader exactly what you mean." Petra nodded. "I like *kind*," she said. "I'm adding that in."

Encourage students to revise their pieces, replacing ordinary words with words that best describe the idea or subject.

"Let's all do the revision Petra showed us to do in our own writing. Go back to your nominations to reread and find places you can find just-right words that show your reader exactly what you mean—words that are much fancier and describe your idea in clearer ways!" I moved across the rug to help students tackle this revision work.

You'll want your students to see each other's advice as helpful—not hurtful. Daily partner time and using student writing during share sessions help students to view each other as caring teachers.

Instead of letting one child's writing become the sole focus of the share, turn the children's attention back to their own writing before calling the workshop to a close.

Session 15

Giving Readers Signposts and Rest Stops

M ANY TEACHERS KNOW WELL Lev Vygotsky's theory of zones of proximal development, the idea that children learn best and most fully when you teach them what they are ready to learn. This zone can feel elusive though. How can we know what is in a child's zone? Donald Bear says that you must look for what children are "using but confusing." In other words, look at your students' work and look for the things they are attempting to do but are not yet doing well. Bear uses this method to assess spelling. If children are representing short vowel sounds in their spelling but using the wrong letters to represent them, they are ready to learn about spelling with short vowels. If, instead, the children have no vowels at all in their spelling—as you can observe in much kindergarten writing—those children are not yet ready to learn about short vowels in spelling. Using but confusing can be a very useful assessment of what to teach—especially when it comes to spelling and grammar.

Chances are that if you have taught second grade before, you have a seen a big shift in your students' sentence structure just about mid-year. Students can be doing a pretty good job of punctuating their sentences in the first portion of the year, then almost overnight (sometime around Presidents' Day) it seems that every sentence has become a run-on! Most teachers start to teach children how to chop their sentences up into smaller, simpler ones, but this goes against the grain of what the children are trying to do. The children are using but confusing longer sentences, so we must teach them how to use longer sentences in a way that works. Earlier in the year, during the *Lessons from the Masters* unit, you taught your students to handle less sophisticated long sentences—a string of sentences connected with the word *and*. Then your teaching was about using end punctuation thoughtfully. Here, you will take on the exciting work of helping children smooth and connect sentences using a variety of punctuation that lives in the middle of the sentence.

In today's session, you'll take a pause from the idea work of this unit and conduct a guided inquiry with your students, and celebrate that your writers are ready for internal punctuation!

IN THIS SESSION, you'll teach students that writers use mid-sentence punctuation to help highlight ideas for their readers.

GETTING READY

✔ Your own nomination writing, enlarged on chart paper. Be sure that it contains a few longer sentences that employ middle of the sentence punctuation, such as commas, dashes, and parentheses (see Guided Inquiry).

✔ Chart paper, divided into three columns, with the headings "What Does It Look Like?" "What Should We Call It?" and "When Can We Use It?" (see Guided Inquiry)

✔ Students' writing folders and pencils (see Link)

✔ Revision strips (see Link)

✔ "How Did I Make My Writing Easy to Read?" section of the Grade 2 Opinion Writing Checklist (see Conferring and Small-Group Work)

✔ Adhesive labels and colored pencils (see Share)

Giving Readers Signposts and Rest Stops

CONNECTION

Gather your writers and explain how longer sentences need some rest stops.

"Last night I was reading your nomination writing. You know, one of the things that impressed me the most was your sentences. Back at the beginning of the year you all wrote these very short simple sentences, but when I was reading last night I was pleased to see how long and fabulous your sentences are becoming! Some of them are as long as three or four lines!

I take this opportunity to point out the growth my students have made as writers, hoping to imbue them with a sense of pride and renewed engagement.

"When you start to write longer sentences, one thing that you need to think about is letting your reader have some rest stops. Think of it this way. When a runner runs a short race, she can run as hard as she can the whole way at full speed. But when a runner runs a marathon, she needs to pace herself. She needs to have rest stops to get a drink and splash some water on her face. I bet you have seen marathon runners grabbing water from someone along the side of the race. She slows down a bit, drinks the water and then keeps on going.

Using an analogy helps students to understand the reason behind your teaching.

"That is kind of how sentences work, too. When you read a long sentence, the reader needs rest stops, like a marathon runner; which means you as a writer need some punctuation in the middle of that long and fabulous sentence. So today we are going to look at punctuation that gives your reader some rest stops in the middle of your sentence."

I listened in as children whispered about using commas and knew that this lesson was perfect for them.

Name the question that will guide the inquiry.

"Today, I am not going to be the one teaching you. I am going to be learning right beside you! Together, we will look over some writing, noticing punctuation *all over*. As we're reading and noticing, we'll be investigating. We'll be detectives, just like Nate the Great! We'll be punctuation detectives, looking to answer the question "What kinds of jobs are rest stop punctuation doing?"

Posing a question at the beginning of an inquiry lesson gives the children a clear focus for what they'll study.

GUIDED INQUIRY

Invite your writers to notice some rest stop punctuation in a few well-written sentences. Guide them through the steps of first noticing the punctuation and then asking themselves what the purpose of the punctuation is.

"Long sentences can help the reader connect parts of the sentence. Let's take a look at a few sentences that do this well. Remember, you will be on the lookout for punctuation in the middle of the sentence. When you see some put your thumb up."

I revealed a sentence from my nomination that I had written on a chart paper. I read it out loud and gave the children a minute to look at it. Then I invited them to talk to their partners.

> The scenes in <u>Pinky and Rex and the Bully</u> are very suspenseful—especially when Pinky first meets the bully (because I didn't know what the bully was going to do next).

I give children time to talk to partners before sharing what they notice. This gives them time to clarify and articulate their thinking before sharing. Plus, it ensures that all children have an audience for their ideas!

As the children talked, I leaned in closer. I was listening for children who might describe the punctuation in ways other kids would understand. Once I coached a few students, I turned back to the class. "What do you notice about the rest stop punctuation, and what kind of jobs do you see it doing?"

Levi began the conversation. "I see a dash, right there, in the middle."

"Great observation. A dash! So now that you've seen it, you need to ask yourself what you think it is doing," I coached. "Uh, it is there and then the writer says more. I think it means that you are saying more about the part before it."

Record punctuation observations in a class chart.

"You got it, Levi! Let's get this information down so we can remember the dash's job and then use it in our own writing." I turned to a sheet of chart paper, where I had already begun a chart that would help us keep track of what we were noticing during our inquiry.

Don't be afraid to make a sophisticated grammar chart like this one. Even if children don't describe the punctuation perfectly, you can revisit the chart, changing and adding to the descriptions over time.

What Does It Look Like?	What Should We Call It?	When Can We Use It?
—	dash	• Use it to say more about the writing that comes before it.

"Good start! What else do you notice here?" Dante's arm shot into the air, and I nodded at him. "The curve lines are there. They are adding."

I looked at the sentence and touched the parentheses. "Do you mean these lines?" Dante's head nodded vigorously as he smiled. "Writers call those *parentheses*. What kind of adding on do you think they are doing? Let me read it to you again so you can think about it." This time I read it a little more dramatically with the parenthetical phrase sounding a little sneaky.

Dante jumped right back in. "You're giving away a little secret in the sentence." He cupped his hands around his mouth to show what he meant. The class laughed in agreement, and Eldin added, "Yeah you're talking smirky."

I added the parentheses to the chart too.

( )	parentheses	• Use them before and after giving away a little secret. • Use them when you want to say something smirky.

"Let's look at another sentence." I read the next sentence out loud, and waited for the whispers.

> Pinky and Rex face problems that many of us know about, like bullies, spelling bees, new neighbors, and siblings.

I nodded at Calder. "I see a bunch of commas, is that the name? And they're all in a row, and in a list," he stated.

Bea raised her hand. "I see the commas too. They're in the list because it is still the same sentence but the reader needs to take a breath and stop. I guess it is like the runner who runs a long time." Bea looked up to the ceiling in thought and then back at me. "I guess it is like a pause but not a stop."

"I thought commas were only for making a list though!" Petra called out.

"I guess what we are learning today is that punctuation can do different jobs in different sentences," I said. "Let's add both of those uses to our chart, and as we read and write we can add more!" I quickly added the commas to our chart and put my marker down.

,	comma	• Use it to give the reader a pause. • Use it to separate items in a list.

LINK

Before sending students off, give them a chance to try rest-stop punctuation in their own fabulous writing.

"Second-graders, we have some great new ideas about punctuation, and now it is time to put them to use! Take out your writing, your pens, and the flaps that I tucked into each of your folders." I paused while the children picked up

If a child notices something but is having a hard time talking about it, you can simply reread to help the child think. If the child is still not sure, add in a turn and talk, then coach children toward an understanding of what they see.

The ultimate goal of this lesson is to help children realize that punctuation is flexible and useful in many different ways.

their writing and gathered everything in their laps. "I know you're dying to reread your writing now and find or write a fabulous sentence that's ready for this new, more sophisticated punctuation work. Go ahead, reread and figure out how you can use your new punctuation powers to add rests for your reader." I moved around the rug quickly, helping the children find a place to start their work.

When I saw many of the children with their finger on the spot they wanted to work on, looking at me expectantly, I said. "Go ahead, go ahead, you know what to do! Try some of the punctuation! Use the flap if you need space to rewrite the sentence, or just add the punctuation right into your writing. Or go ahead and try a brand new fabulous sentence, with rest stops along the way!"

Remind the class that punctuation is one way to take care of your reader.

"Writers, whenever you write, you want to take care of your reader, and punctuation is one of the tools you can use to help your reader. Your reader is going to be so happy with these little rest stops, not just today, but whenever you write longer sentences. Off you go!"

This will not be the last time you talk to students about middle of the sentence (or median) punctuation. Remember that this teaching will likely need to be followed by small groups and conferences to continue and clarify this work.

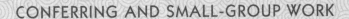

Teaching Past the "Using but Confusing" Stage

THE IDEA OF LOOKING for what a child is using but confusing can be a great way to teach children to edit their own work too. All too often, teachers fall into the trap of editing students' writing for them. Or teachers look through a child's writing and circle everything that needs to be "fixed." While this does set the child up to edit, it does not give the child an opportunity to practice *finding* misspellings and convention errors.

You might try pulling together a group of writers and showing them how to *find* and then fix their editing challenges (remember to position these as exciting challenges and not amenable errors). One way to do this is to gather a group of children who want to use harder words and often misspell words from your word wall. You might have a small copy of the word wall for each child to hold and mark up. Be sure that children have their writing folders with them, not just one piece of writing. You might start the group by telling the children that we can make our writing easier to read by studying the words we write often and then using the word wall to help spell them. The children can look across the word wall, thinking, "Which of these words that are hard for me do I use but confuse?" This is a great way to make checking for spelling manageable. When we teach children to spell high-frequency words, sometimes they do not stick. This is often because while the word may be used frequently across the English language, it is not a word the child uses often. Other times something is going on in that child's brain that makes spelling challenging. They'll have to work extra hard at this. And often spelling will *never* be easy for these children, so it's going to take a lot of stamina. The children can use a highlighter to indicate which words they need to focus on. Have the children in your group look through their writing to find those words and then fix them up using the mini–word wall as a spelling guide.

MID-WORKSHOP TEACHING **An Editing Break**

"Writers, can I have your attention please? We'll take a break from writing *more*, so that we can look for ways to make our writing clearer and easier to read. Today, since we just learned ways to make our longer sentences clearer, you will probably want to check for that! In fact, let's do that now.

"Christopher just suggested that he take a break as a writer. Well, I was shocked, children! A break? We don't take breaks, we keep writing!" I winked at the children.

"Then Christopher explained that he wanted to fix some stuff up in his writing. 'I need an Editing Break,' he said. Isn't that a good idea? Let's try it.

"Look back at your piece and reread what you've already written. Look for those longer, more fabulous sentences. Thumbs up when you find one!" After a few moments, I prompted students to take the next step. "Great, now reread it and ask, 'Is this clear?' If it isn't, go ahead and try one of the strategies we practiced today. You can work on this for a minute or two." I moved from table to table as students worked to edit their more sophisticated sentences. Then, I encouraged the students to work with a partner to make a final check.

"Will you turn to your partner and read your fabulous sentence out loud? Partners, listen closely and look carefully to make sure there are marks on the page that signal for the reader to take a rest stop along the way. If something is missing, help your partner find a place to add it."

You can teach small groups of this manner for many conventions. Perhaps you'll give the children a list of conventions and then have them highlight the ones they use but confuse and then read through their writing to fix this up. By having the children start with the questions "What do I find I find hard? What do I use but confuse?" you can help them to focus their editing efforts on aspects of editing that will help them the most. At this point in the unit, you might simply pull out the "How did I make my writing easy to read?" portion of the Opinion Writing checklist for Grade 2.

The children could then read over the items on the checklist and ask, "Which of these is a habit for me now, and which do I still have to think about?" They could highlight those items that they need to think about and check them at the end of each workshop time or during an editing break.

	How Did I Make My Writing Easy to Read?
• Spelling	• To spell a word, I used what I know about similar words. • Sometimes the word wall helped.
• Punctuation	• I used a capital letter for names. • I used quotation marks to show what people said. • When I used words like *can't* and *don't*, I put in the apostrophe.

And the Award Goes to . . .

Working with Committees to Determine the Winners

Have students bring their two best nomination writing pieces to the share session. Divide them into small groups to "judge" the nominations, and select the one piece that will be showcased at the upcoming writing celebration.

"Boys and girls, I have a big announcement to make. But before you come over, look across all the nominations you've collected in your folder and choose two pieces that show off everything you know about opinion writing. Pick your very best and most convincing nominations and bring them to your spot on the rug."

I ushered the students to join me in the meeting area with their chosen nominations in hand. Once the class had settled, I leaned in and whispered with glee, "You have collected so many nominations for some of the very best books that you think deserve awards. It is almost time to announce the winners! But, guess what the best part is?"

The students leaned forward, awaiting the news. I went on to announce, "*You* will be the judges! You will work together in small committees to decide which nomination is the *most* convincing of all. This way, each of you will have one book to showcase at our book fair celebration in a few days." The class applauded the news.

"So, right now. Let's get into groups of four. You'll each have a turn to read aloud the nominations that show off your best work. Now judges, your job will be to listen extra closely to the reasons and details in each nomination to decide which nominee should be showcased at our book fair. Pick the writing that is the most convincing!"

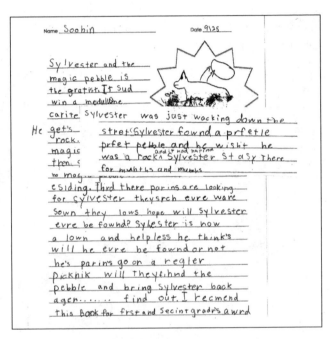

FIG. 15–1   Soobin chooses a piece she has revised.

The children quickly formed small groups, spreading out across the rug. I voiced over to remind students of the strategies they'd been learning across the entire unit. "Be sure to listen for writing that shows off these strategies, before you vote for which is the strongest."

Ask students to think about an award that best fits the attributes of the book, to capture the attention of a selective audience of readers.

Once the groups had selected the best nominees, I explained the final task. "Judges, you've looked over the nominees and selected the best of the best. But now that you've decided which books deserve an award, you'll need to decide *what* kind of award best fits.

"Book awards," I explained, "grab the attention of readers. They have names like Funniest Book or 'Make You Cry' Book. The kind of award you give can determine the kind of reader who finds it. Think carefully about your nominee. What kind of reader do you hope will find your book? What is special about your book that makes it important to read? Perhaps, you'll think about the genre, or the best qualities, or the big lesson of the story to help you come up with the name of your award.

"Meet with your committee to share ideas about the name of the awards you'll give your book. Once you have your award name ready, head back to your tables. I'll pass around special label paper for you to design your award. You'll use these to honor your books at the celebration." The students used colored pencils and adhesive label cutouts to quickly design their award emblems.

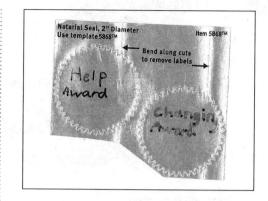

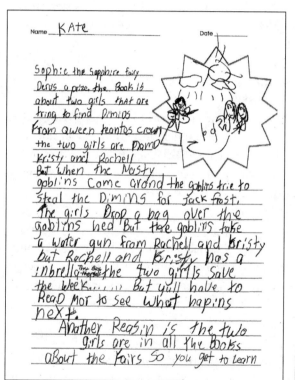

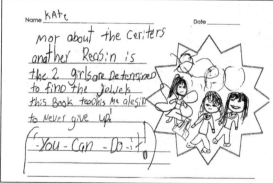

FIG. 15–2   Kate chooses a piece with several reasons in it.

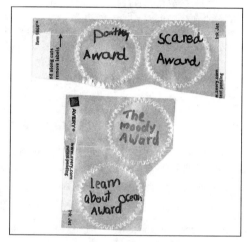

FIG. 15–3   Students make award stickers for each other's books.

Writing Introductions and Conclusions to Captivate

IN THIS SESSION, you'll teach students that writers read and study the work of other writers and then try to incorporate what they have learned into their own writing. In this case, the focus will be on writing introductions and conclusions.

GETTING READY

✔ Mentor text enlarged on chart paper, as well as individual copies for students (see Connection and Guided Inquiry)

✔ Clipboards and highlighter markers (see Guided Inquiry)

✔ Post-it notes (see Guided Inquiry)

✔ Chart paper with labeled Venn diagram, one circle for introductions and the other for conclusions (see Guided Inquiry)

✔ Revision flaps and strips in the writing center (see Link)

✔ Student writing from early in the year, preferably from the first day of school, when they did on-demand writing (see Share)

O NE OF THE MOST REMARKABLE ASPECTS of world-class standards is how, as you look up the grade levels at the skill sets defined for writing narrative, opinion, and information texts, there is schema that stays the same, no matter what the type of writing. For instance, regardless of the genre, the standards emphasize the importance of crafting beginnings that set a clear focus for a piece of writing and introduce the subject to the reader. Similar skill sets exist for elaboration and for endings. This is incredibly helpful to our teaching. It reminds us to say to our young writers, "No matter what kind of writing you are making, it's always helpful to think about how your beginning introduces things to the reader, how the middle elaborates, and how the ending brings it all to a close." Whether you are telling a story, teaching something, or explaining an opinion, you always want to provide your readers with the same things. You always want to give them a beginning, a middle, and an end.

Up until this point in the unit, you have taught your writers a great deal about the middle, about the meat of the writing, about the elaboration. You have taught them to find meaningful opinions and ideas and to add to those opinions with details and quotes from their books. You have taught them how to make their opinions clear and convincing. Now, it is time to teach them to introduce those ideas and then draw them to a close. It is time to teach beginnings and endings in opinion writing.

In this session, you will invite your students to take a look at a mentor text. Through the inquiry process, your students will discover that introductions and conclusions include many of the same elements. They both tend to give the title of the book and the author and illustrator's names. They both tend to state an opinion. They both tend to talk straight to the reader, asking questions or giving suggestions. But they also have several distinct differences. You will want to be sure that your writers notice that introductions draw in the reader. You will want them to see that an introduction has to be interesting and engaging, and in this case it will need to catch the attention of a serious judge. On the other hand, you will want them to notice that a conclusion has to pull it all together, like a ribbon around a package, and then send the reader off—hopefully to read this fabulous book. We call it "catch and hold!"

Writing Introductions and Conclusions to Captivate

CONNECTION

Tell children that you are impressed with their nomination writing and all of the strategies that they are using to make their pieces powerful and persuasive.

The children gathered at the meeting area, each bringing along a highlighter marker and clipboard as instructed. I asked the class to put their materials aside for the moment. Then, I began by celebrating the growth they had made as opinion writers, drawing upon an expanding repertoire of strategies.

"Boys and girls, I've been admiring you these past few days. You are doing everything you know to write nominations that convince readers that the books you love the most are books that deserve awards! You're including reasons and details to support your opinion. You're making comparisons and finding evidence in your books to prove your ideas. You're even using quotation marks to add the exact words from the text. You are growing in such impressive ways as opinion writers! You know just what to do to convince your audience. And well you should since, after all, you've been writing about your opinions since kindergarten! Pat yourselves on the back!" The students turned toward each other, sharing in the pride of having done such evolved work.

"So, since you just keep getting smarter and stronger as opinion writers, what if we spend some time, right now, getting *even* smarter? Are you up for it?" I propositioned. The class let out a resounding, "Yes!"

Explain that opinion writers have the challenge of catching the attention of their audience and communicating their claims, before releasing them.

"The stories you love the most have a beginning that captures your attention and begs you to turn the page, and an ending that stays with you, even after the book has been put back on the shelf. Just like the beginnings and endings of your favorite books catch and hold you, opinion writing begins with an introduction to catch readers' attention and a conclusion that holds readers and keeps them thinking." As I named this process, I used gestures to clarify the analogy of catching and holding, as if I were catching and holding a ball.

"I have a nomination, right here, that I find convincing. Let's study this piece together to learn ways *we* can write introductions to begin our pieces in captivating ways and conclusions that end our pieces in memorable ways." I quickly distributed the student copies and then turned to an enlarged version I had placed on the easel.

This kind of connection, in which you remind children of all they've learned, is one you can use for any minilesson.

Notice how we make a connection between narrative writing and opinion writing here. You will find that helping children to see the similarities in different kinds of writing promotes transfer from unit to unit.

✤ **Name the inquiry question.**

"This means that, once again, I am not teaching you something, because instead, we'll discover the answers together. After all, you've already been working to become your own teachers. So, let's think about this big question: 'What do nomination writers do to introduce and conclude their piece in captivating ways?' Then, we'll be able to ask, 'How can we do this in our nominations, too?'"

GUIDED INQUIRY

Set writers up to investigate a mentor text by guiding them through a series of steps that help students discover answers to the overarching question. Then listen in and coach, to elicit and collect their comments.

"Okay, writers, the first thing we'll need to do is to find places in this nomination that we think catch our attention. I'll read the beginning aloud. Listen carefully. When you hear a part that grabs your attention, give me a signal and we'll highlight those words or lines so that we can go back and study them more carefully." I read the nomination line by line, while students held onto their own copies, highlighters in hand.

> *"She is such a nice girl, you should be friends." Parents are* **always** *saying that. But who wants to be friends with someone your parents choose for you?* **YUCK!** *Well, that is just how Bean feels at the beginning of this picture-filled chapter book that is perfect for second graders. Ivy and Bean, written by Annie Barrows and illustrated by Sophie Blackall, should get the Best Friends Don't Have to Be Just Alike Award. Bean's mother tries to convince her to be friends with Ivy, but Bean likes to play tricks on people and stand on her head. She doesn't want to be friends with Ivy. Ivy is the new girl who lives across the street and wears pretty dresses and sparkly headbands. But soon enough, Bean learns that just because they are different doesn't mean they can't find ways to have tons of fun together! With potions, magic spells and secret plans, these two girls become the* **bestest** *of best friends.*

I paused to think aloud. "Hmm. What does this writer do to catch our attention right from the start of the piece?" I left a space for students to think independently, disregarding raised hands for the moment.

"Now, let's read on to explore how this writer ends the piece with a conclusion that keeps us thinking." I read on.

> *Once Barrow and Blackall finished Ivy and Bean they must have realized it was just too good of a book not to write more stories about these two friends. After you finish reading this first book, you should read the whole series! Ivy and Bean is perfect for the Best Friends Don't Have to Be Just Alike Award, because while the girls do become friends, they never become alike. This is no ordinary everyone-should-be-friends book.* **NO WAY!** *This book helps you to see that if you look a little deeper, someone who seems different, might actually the perfect friend for you. Why not share Ivy and Bean with your best friend?*

You are welcome to use this piece, authored for this purpose. You could just as easily choose to share your own writing or the writing of a past student here. Remember, the idea is to teach children that they can study any piece of successful writing in an effort to improve their own writing skills.

If you worry that it is too much to teach introductions and conclusions in this way, you might choose to structure this lesson differently. Instead, you can craft a standard demonstration lesson in which you tell children the attributes an introduction should have (and then model adding these to your writing), then introduce a few attributes that conclusions have, letting children practice incorporating these into their own writing.

"It is easy to tell that this writer feels quite strongly about this book, giving many reasons and details to support her opinion. But what's especially important when writing a nomination is persuading the judges right from the start and holding onto their attention until the very end of the piece. Let's study the piece with a partner to answer our big question, 'What do nomination writers do to introduce and conclude their piece in captivating ways?' As you reread it with your partner, be sure to highlight sentences that you think will help you to answer this question."

Coach children to study structure, voice, word choice, and craft as they work in pairs.

As children worked, I voiced over, "The answers are not always so easy to find. You can look back across the words and lines you highlighted and ask yourself, 'What is it about this part that makes it so captivating?'"

I left a moment for students to do this inquiry work independently. Then, I said, "Writers, point to one thing that the writer did to catch your attention at the beginning, or keep your attention at the end. Think about what *exactly* makes that part stand out. What did the writer do that we can try, too?" Eager arms rose up across the rug. Some children held up their copies, exposing lines of bright yellow. "Turn and share what you notice with your partner."

Listen in and highlight observations that students make.

I crouched beside Sam and Lily to listen in. "There are words that pop out, like, *Yuck*. See, because it's all capital," he said, pointing to his copy of the text.

"And bold, too," Lily noted.

"That makes those words really stand out, almost as if they are popping off the page. Did she do that anywhere else?" I nudged.

"Here!" Sam remarked, pointing down the page.

"And here, too!" Lily noted, returning to the first line of the text. "But here it's not capital, it's just bold."

"That's because you have to read it in a special way and make it stand out," Sam explained, reading aloud to emphasize the proper intonation. I moved on to another partnership to make note of the other observations children were making.

Reconvene the group to elicit students' observations. Repeat their observations using more precise language, and record these on sticky notes to add to a Venn diagram chart.

"Writers, I'm hearing so many smart observations about the introduction and conclusion in this nomination. Let's make a chart to list the strategies the writer probably used to catch readers' attention. Then, we can challenge ourselves to try these strategies in our nominations, too." As students made suggestions, I named them in clearer and more concise ways as I recorded them on sticky notes.

Notice how I restate the guided inquiry question again before having the children turn and talk. This is to ensure that the talk is focused. You may find that as you listen in you need to say the question again as a way to coach student talk.

Coaching students to find more examples of one strategy is a useful way to get them to think more deeply about the author's intent in using the strategy.

"The name of the book and the author is in it so the reader can know what the nomination is about," Levi offered.

"You are right! The writer makes sure to include the title and author. Is that included in the introduction or in the conclusion? Or in both places in the piece?" The children quickly scanned their copies.

"Both!" the class shouted back.

I quickly jotted "Title and author" on a sticky note and added it to the middle of our Venn diagram chart. "So, this is something we can try in both our introductions and our conclusions. Great! What else?"

"She put the name of the award, too. The Best Friends Don't Have to Be Alike Award!" Petra giggled. "Oh, and she put it in the conclusion, too!" she added on, predicting my next question. I quickly added this to the middle of our chart.

"Plus, she asked a question right to the reader," Dante piped in.

"Almost, as if she's talking right to us? That's a sure way to grab the reader's attention!" I noted, adding to the list.

"She told a little bit about the story. But she didn't give everything away and spoil the ending, like my sister does when she sees a movie. She only retells the most important things to know about the story," Audrey commented.

"Let's all look back to find what Audrey is describing. Do you see where the writer included a sneak peek of the book?" I gave the class a moment to locate this detail. Then, I went on, "Now can you find evidence of a sneak peek in the conclusion, or is this something writers do mostly at the beginning?" Again, I gave the students some time to study the mentor text.

"It's mostly in the introduction. But the conclusion has the big lesson of the story," Christopher observed.

"You're right about that. It's almost like the sneak peek at the beginning pulls us in. But the conclusion is the writer's chance to add some final words to wrap it all up. It's a catch and release!" I jotted these observations onto sticky notes, then placed them in the corresponding parts of the charted diagram.

I continued eliciting students' observations to compose a menu of strategies for composing catchy introductions and thought-provoking conclusions.

You will want to be sure that your children notice what is included in both the introduction and the conclusion. By noticing these similarities they come to better understand the circular nature of these two parts of writing.

If students do not offer observations about techniques that are unique to either introductions or conclusions, you can guide their attention toward it. You might say, "Hmm . . . I liked this part . . . What do you think the author was doing here? Is it in both the introduction and the conclusion, or just one?"

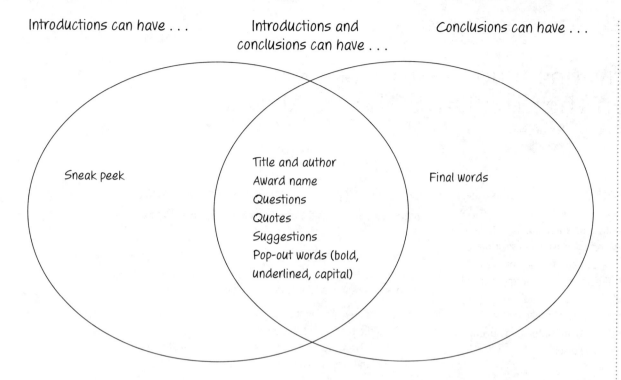

Introductions can have . . .

Introductions and conclusions can have . . .

Conclusions can have . . .

Sneak peek

Title and author
Award name
Questions
Quotes
Suggestions
Pop-out words (bold, underlined, capital)

Final words

You can anticipate that children will make note of different details across this mentor text and, of course, across other examples. The Venn diagram option for this chart can create an opportunity for you to study how the overlap in this example may not be equivalent in other pieces. The important understanding you'll want to communicate to your students is that writers draw from a repertoire of possible strategies, exploring ways to strengthen their introductions and conclusions, to spark immediate interest and end their pieces with a strong sense of closure.

"Wow, such a smart list! I bet that list you have up in your mind, or tucked away in your back pocket, is getting longer and longer as you become stronger opinion writers." The children nodded and giggled, some stretching imaginary lists from their pockets and heads.

"I'm wondering how many of you might challenge yourself to do this kind of work to catch and hold onto your readers' attention." Arms rose up enthusiastically.

LINK

Send writers off to work independently, reminding them to call on prior knowledge as well as what they have learned today about writing introductions and conclusions.

"Nomination writers, it's time for you to get started. Remember, when you write your pieces, you'll write using all that you already know about opinion writing," I began, gesturing toward the anchor chart in the room. "But you will also try to do some of this very grown-up and challenging work that nomination writers in the world do to convince the committee of judges who read their entries—catching their attention at the very start and ending their piece in ways they'll remember.

"There are lots of revision flaps and strips in the writing center to help you do this work, adding introductions and conclusions to the nominations across your whole folder! Remember to look back at this chart we created together to help you as you work independently. Off you go!"

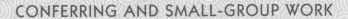
Motivating Students to Make Revisions when They Think that They're All Done

INTRODUCTIONS ARE NOT COMPLETELY NEW TERRITORY for your students. After all, they touched on them in first grade and wrote some for their information books earlier this year. Because of this prior work with introductions, there are likely to be a fair number of children who have small introductions and conclusions in their pieces already. While many children will instantly see that they can add to and change their beginnings, there will also be children who say, "I already have an introduction. I already did my conclusion. I'm all set!" Motivating these children to take on further revision, adding on and saying even more, can sometimes be a challenge. In these moments, it is key to remember that we want to feed the student's internal motivation and not bluntly say, "Well you have to do more, because I said so."

This was an issue I faced when I spoke to Lexie. As I looked over at Lexie, she was shuffling through her nominations. I approached her. "Hi Lexie, what are you working on today?"

"Oh, I'm looking through my nominations," she replied quickly. I noticed a hint of "leave me alone" in her voice. "I have them already, so I'm done, I'm all set."

"Let's take a longer look. Which of these nominations do you think is your very best? The one you know will absolutely convince the judges to give it an award?" Lexie shuffled her papers a bit more and then pulled out her piece about Judy Moody (see Figure 16–1). I knew she really loved this book, and she had done a nice job with this writing already—including examples and quotes and using revision strips to add in a lesson, even some little pictures, like the extras we added to our letters at the end of the last bend. I asked Lexie to read the introduction to me, so that we could think about how to draw her reader in even more. As I read over her shoulder, I noted that she did, in fact, have an introduction of sorts as well as a bit of a conclusion. But it was clear that both could benefit from some revision work. And more importantly, I needed to convince her, as a writer, that revision would be worth her while.

MID-WORKSHOP TEACHING   Writing and Revising Introductions and Conclusions: Partner Work

"Writers, can I have your eyes and ears over here for a moment, please? I see folders open and revision flaps out. It seems that so many of you are finding nominations and adding introductions or revising conclusions. Impressive!

"I want to remind you that an introduction is the writer's first opportunity to talk to the reader, and the conclusion is the last chance to convince him or her. So, it is important to catch their attention from the very first line and hold on until the very last word.

"Who better is there to help us know if we are writing in ways that talk right to our readers than our partners? Let's team up and read our introductions and conclusions to one another. Partner 1 you'll start. Partner 2, your job will be to listen and decide if the introduction and conclusion grab your attention and use words that talk right to you. If not, you can work together to explore other ways it could go, and then revise. Let's spend the rest of our workshop time working with our partners to make our introductions and conclusions even more captivating!" I moved from one partnership to another, coaching in to support this collaboration.

"Lexie, I know how much you love this Judy Moody book. Now, imagine for a moment that a judge is sitting at her desk with a pile of nominations in front of her. She is reading through them and she is starting to get tired. She has been reading these nominations *all* day. You want her to pick yours up and open up her eyes and ears! What would you say to her? What could you write that would wake her up and make her think, 'Oh this sound fabulous, exciting. This book just *has to* get an award!'"

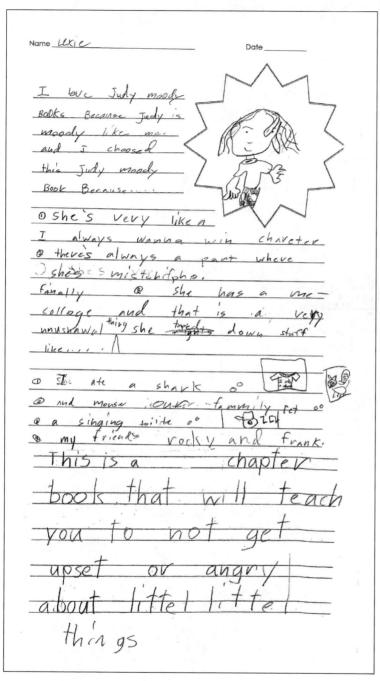

Name Lexie   Date _____

I love Judy moody
Books Because Judy is
moody like me.
and I choosed
this Judy moody
Book Because....

① She's very like a
I always wanna win charveter
② there's always a part where
) she's mistchifpho.
Fanally ③ she has a me-
collage and that is a very
unushawal thing she tryes down stuff
like.... .

① She ate a shark °°
② and mouse ourer fammily pet °°
③ a singing toilite °° ZLA
④ my friends rocky and frank.
This is a   chapter
book that will teach
you to not get
upset or angry
about littel littel
things

FIG. 16–1   Lexie's nomination before conference

Lexie considered this for a minute, deciding whether she would add to her writing, then in a newly excited voice said, "Judy Moody is the moodiest kid you will ever meet! She is funny and rude, but she is good, too." I pushed her to say even more, reminding her to say it as though she were talking directly to the judge.

After another minute, I summed up the strategy that Lexie used, to ensure that it would be something that she could take with her beyond this piece of writing. "Lexie, when I came over here, you thought you were all finished, and now look at this great plan you have for what to do to make your writing even better!" I handed Lexie a revision strip and continued on. "I am glad to see you excited to add more. Remember how we talked about rehearsing to increase our energy for writing when we were working on letters?" Lexie nodded. "Well, I think that talking to rehearse is just what you needed to get excited and back to work! Promise me that you'll remember that next time."

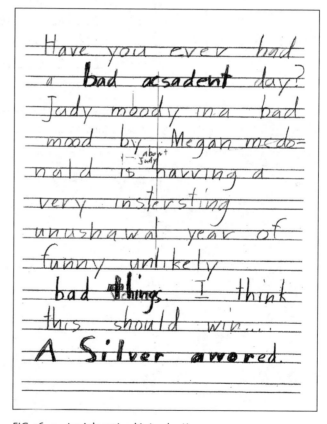

Have you ever had
a bad acsadent day?
Judy moody in a bad
mood by Megan mcdo-
nald is havving a
very instersting
unushawal year of
funny unlikely
bad things. I think
this should win...
A Silver awored.

FIG. 16–2   Lexie's revised introduction

Name ___Lexie___   Date _____

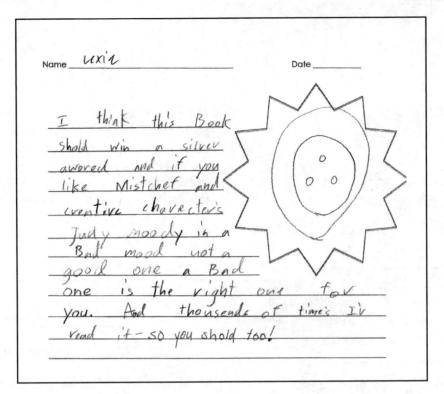

I think this Book
shold win a silver
awored and if you
like Mistchef and
crentive charecter's
Judy moody in a
Bad mood not a
good one a Bad
one is the right one for
you. And thouseads of time's I'v
read it—so you shold too!

FIG. 16–3   Lexie's added conclusion

Wow! Look How We've Grown! Reflecting on Writing to Celebrate Progress and Set Goals

Give them an old piece of writing to compare to their current writing, and ask them to look at specific characteristics when comparing the two pieces.

"Writers, will you come to the rug with your whole writing folder?" The children gathered and I looked at them. They were so grown-up, and I wanted them to know it. As they sat down, I revealed that I was holding something dear in my arms, but I kept secret what it was. "Writers, today we are going to take a moment to talk about then and now. We are going to take a minute to marvel at all you can do and how much you have grown. I want you to know that in just a portion of a school year, you have gone from little kids who still needed help tying shoes and finding the office, to the big kids who sit before me, who help kindergartners open doors and can deliver notes all over the building.

"But your growing is not just about knowing your school and helping little kids. You have grown as writers, too! In my hands, I have the writing you did on the first day of school. It is lovely and sweet, but it is definitely little kid writing." With this I handed out all of the on-demand pieces children had written at the start of the year. The children started to talk instantly, laughing and joking about how big the letters were and how short the writing was. Some didn't quite believe it was theirs at all.

"Writers, you are already sharing your writing with your friends, and that is exactly what we will be doing for the share today. But will you give me your attention for just one minute?" I paused and waited until I had everyone's attention and then continued on. "Let's have a way of looking at this writing. Let's decide that as we look at this writing, we will think about then and now. Choose something specific to look at in your First Day writing, and then look at the same thing in your writing now. For example, maybe you will look at your First Day writing and notice your sentences. Perhaps they were only four or five words long. Then, take a look at the sentences in your current writing. What do you notice? Talk with your partner about your growth. You might say, 'Back then I wrote sentences that had four or five words, and now I have some sentences with ten words and lots of resting punctuation.' Be sure to take turns so that you both get lots of chances." I had barely finished my sentence, and the children were off and running. I moved around the classroom, reminding kids to feel their own pride and pat themselves on the back.

"Wow, writers you certainly have grown in so many ways! Give yourselves a pat on the back!" I waited while the children congratulated themselves. "Writers, remember that as we grow, we always want to get better too, right? So tomorrow, we are going to take all these great feelings we have about growing up and use them to grow some more, because tomorrow we will come up with brand-new writing goals!"

If you have your on-demand opinion writing from the start of the year, use that. If not, the first day of this unit will do.

Using a Checklist to Set Writerly Goals

IN THIS SESSION, you'll teach students that writers use tools to help them evaluate their writing, figure out what they are doing well, and then make a plan for what they want to do better.

GETTING READY

✔ Your own familiar demonstration text, to model using the checklist, enlarged for students to see (see Teaching)

✔ Opinion Writing Checklist, Grades 2 and 3, enlarged, as well as individual copies for students (see Teaching, Active Engagement, and Mid-Workshop Teaching)

✔ Post-it notes, in two different colors. We use green and pink (see Teaching and Active Engagement)

✔ Index cards for students to write their goals on (see Active Engagement)

✔ Plain white paper for mini-charts (see Conferring and Small-Group Work and Share)

MOTIVATING WRITERS is always part of the work we do. In the last sessions, we worked hard to allow *our* energy and zeal for hard work to influence *the children's* energy and zeal for hard work. In this session, you will rely more heavily on developing your students' own sense of agency. Agency is one of the big focuses in teaching (and child rearing) these days. Agency is well developed when children feel confident enough to face a challenging task with a sense of initiative and then believe in their abilities enough to persist through the challenge, thus trying something even when they are unsure that they will succeed. Po Bronson and Ashley Merryman, in their book *Nurture Shock*, share research that suggests that merely praising kids—telling them they are smart, for example—may build their self-esteem. But if that praise focuses on the child, rather than the *actions* of the child, it can have the adverse effect of dulling the child's sense of agency. In other words, if you tell a child she is smart, she will think, "If I try something new and fail, I will show that I am not smart, and therefore, I should not even try." However, if you compliment a child's actions—"Wow! You tried one thing and then another and you figured it out!"—she will think, "If I work and try, I can figure things out. I can make something happen!"

In *Choice Words* (2004), Peter Johnston writes about the particular importance of fostering agency in the classroom. "As teachers, then, we try to maximize children's feelings of agency. There are really three parts to this: the belief that the environment can be affected, the belief that one has what it takes to affect it, and the understanding that this is what literacy is about" (39). Writing workshop is, at its core, a place for agency in the classroom. Here, children develop ideas, reread them, change them, see the effect of their ideas on others, and then write some more.

While agency is a basic tenant of writing workshop, it is the particular focus of this session. This is a session that will celebrate agency from beginning to end and everywhere in between. Here we will suggest that you can help your children help themselves and then step back a bit and marvel at all they know and can do. We will encourage you to let the children choose their own goals, make their own plans, invent their own strategies and teach each other in the process. This self-assessment, planning, and inventing will not only help your children to feel a sense of ownership in their learning; it will increase their depth of knowledge work to what Norman Webb describes as the highest level (Level 4, extended thinking), in which learners take concepts and ideas they have used in one realm and apply them independently to the work they do in another.

"We will suggest that you can help your children help themselves and then step back a bit and marvel at all they know and can do."

As this session draws to a close, we will further encourage you to have some of your students present their thinking and learning. As they present their strategies to the class, they will also learn to speak clearly and connect learning culled from prior lessons with strategies they developed on their own, and with those of their classmates. By the end of the session, you may have put yourself out of a job entirely!

Using a Checklist to Set Writerly Goals

CONNECTION

Generate excitement for the end of the unit celebration. Explain to students that to get ready to publish, they'll need to make expert decisions about goals for themselves as writers.

"Writers, you've been working hard as opinion writers now for a while, first with letters about books and now with nominations for the books you love the most. You have important choices to make each day as you decide what to work on."

I looked at the children seriously, from one writer to another. "You know, it's sort of a big deal for writers, deciding what to do each day. You might decide to do things in your nominations that you worked on doing in your letters.

"We are getting very close to the end of this unit; in just a few short days, we will have a book fair celebration, where your nomination writing will be on display for all to see, in the hopes of convincing others to love your books just as much as you do. To get your piece ready for publication, you will need to set some goals as a writer. One way to do this is to evaluate the nomination that you think is your best so far. That way, you can figure out the things that you do well and compliment yourself on those things, and then figure out the things you want to work on, so you can set expert goals. Maybe, with help from your partner or classmates, you could work on some of these goals today and for the rest of the week. And then you'll be all ready for the big book fair!"

❖ **Name the teaching point.**

"Today, I want to teach you that writers use tools to help them evaluate their writing, figure out what they are doing well, and then make a plan for what they want to do better. You can use the Opinion Writing Checklist to reflect on your nominations."

◆ COACHING

Teaching children to read their writing and make decisions about what they can do to improve it is very sophisticated work. Let your students know that you are giving them a "grown-up" challenge. You may worry that they are not entirely ready for this. Remind yourself that you are a fostering agency and then send them off to make their decisions.

TEACHING

Use your own nomination writing to demonstrate the process of self-reflection and goal setting. Compare it to the criteria on the Opinion Writing Checklist and make a plan for moving forward.

"So, writers, you probably remember how to do this. We did similar work in our author study and then again when we wrote information books. But before you get started with your own writing, I'm going to walk you through the process, with my writing." I flipped to my *Pinky and Rex* nomination writing, which I had copied onto a sheet of chart paper. I read it aloud to the class.

> Have you ever come face to face with a bully? If you have, you know it can be a big challenge. Pinky from <u>Pinky and Rex and the Bully</u>, by James Howe deals with this tough situation. I think this book deserves the <u>Be True to Yourself Award</u> because it teaches readers this very valuable lesson.
>
> <u>Pinky and Rex and the Bully</u> is a book people absolutely need to read because of the important lessons this story teaches readers, like how you should be true to yourself no matter what others might say. Pinky is picked on by an older kid, named Kevin. Kevin teases Pinky just because of his nickname and because his best friend is a girl! I think Pinky is one of the bravest characters in children's books. He learns to stand up for himself. He's the kind of kid who cares more about being a good friend than what others might say. For example, on page 36 in the story, "Pinky walked straight up to Kevin and poked him in the chest. 'It's none of your business what I like,' he said. 'Or who I play with.'"
>
> Another reason is that the characters you meet in this story are so interesting. Pinky and Rex face problems that many of us know about, for example, bullies, spelling bees, new neighbors, and siblings.
>
> Also, the scenes in <u>Pinky and Rex and the Bully</u> are very suspenseful—especially when Pinky first meets the bully (because I didn't know what the bully was going to do next). It makes you want to turn the page to find out what will happen. It is more suspenseful than the scenes in <u>Pinky and Rex Go to Camp</u>.
>
> You probably agree that <u>Pinky and Rex and the Bully</u> is the best choice for the <u>Be True to Yourself Award</u>! It is an important book for kids of all ages to read. Once you meet Pinky and Rex, you'll want to be friends forever. Well, luckily, there is a whole series of books to read. You should check them out right away!

You could also hand out copies of the writing so students can read along with you. This can help children read more closely and find greater detail.

Your demonstration piece should feel familiar to children from earlier lessons. You might decide to insert a flaw or two, one last thing you think many of your children would benefit from working on. Then, as you judge your piece, you are also modeling revision for specific writers.

"Now, what I'm going to need to do is compare my writing to the Opinion Writing Checklist." I gestured toward the enlarged copy, which was prominently displayed in the writing center. "Remember, this checklist is the list of things that writing teachers decided all second-graders should be able to do by the very end of second grade. We also have a list of things that are expected for writers to do by the end of third grade. Don't worry if some of the things in the third-grade column are a stretch for you. You are still second-graders, right? But I bet you'll realize that many of you are already doing some of the things that third-grade writers are expected to do.

"As I read over the checklist, I'm going to put Post-it notes on my writing. Green Post-it notes will show me, 'Yes, I did this!' and pink Post-it notes will say to me, 'Hold on a sec! I need to fix this or do this better.'" I began to read through the first few bullets of the checklist, evaluating my writing against it.

Model moving between the checklist and your own demonstration text, noting what you've done and have yet to do as an opinion writer.

Opinion Writing Checklist

	Grade 2	NOT YET	STARTING TO	YES!	Grade 3	NOT YET	STARTING TO	YES!
	Structure				**Structure**			
Overall	I wrote my opinion or my likes and dislikes and gave reasons for my opinion.	☐	☐	☐	I told readers my opinion and ideas on a text or a topic and helped them understand my reasons.	☐	☐	☐
Lead	I wrote a beginning in which I not only gave my opinion, but also set readers up to expect that my writing would try to convince them of it.	☐	☐	☐	I wrote a beginning in which I not only set readers up to expect that this would be a piece of opinion writing, but also tried to hook them into caring about my opinion.	☐	☐	☐
Transitions	I connected parts of my piece using words such as *also*, *another*, and *because*.	☐	☐	☐	I connected my ideas and reasons with my examples using words such as *for example* and *because*. I connected one reason or example using words such as *also* and *another*.	☐	☐	☐
Ending	I wrote an ending in which I reminded readers of my opinion.	☐	☐	☐	I worked on an ending, perhaps a thought or comment related to my opinion.	☐	☐	☐
Organization	My piece had different parts; I wrote a lot of lines for each part.	☐	☐	☐	I wrote several reasons or examples of why readers should agree with my opinion and wrote at least several sentences about each reason.	☐	☐	☐
					I organized my information so that each part of my writing was mostly about one thing.	☐	☐	☐
	Development				**Development**			
Elaboration	I wrote at least two reasons and wrote at least a few sentences about each one.	☐	☐	☐	I not only named my reasons to support my opinion, but also wrote more about each one.	☐	☐	☐
Craft	I chose words that would make readers agree with my opinion.	☐	☐	☐	I not only told readers to believe me, but also wrote in ways that got them thinking or feeling in certain ways.	☐	☐	☐

"Let's see. I'm going to read the first part of the checklist and see what plans I can make for my piece overall." I read the Overall category of grade 2 and then grade 3, noting the differences between the two. "Hmm, so am I doing this more like a second-grader, or am I already writing my opinion piece like a third-grader?" I gestured back toward my nomination, pointing toward the specific parts of the text to provide evidence for how the piece reflected third-grade expectations. "I definitely told readers my opinion about the book and helped them understand my reasons with details. I even used quotes to support my reasons." I placed a green Post-it on my piece, jotting, "Overall" on the note to acknowledge that I had done this work well.

I moved on to the "Lead" category of the checklist. "Hmm, does my beginning go like this or like this?" I gestured toward the descriptions of second-grade and third-grade leads. Then, after looking back at my introduction and rereading it aloud, I picked up a pink Post-it note. "I definitely gave my opinion in the beginning of my piece, but I don't think that I let the reader know that this is an opinion piece. The reader might not expect that I'm writing to convince them to agree with my opinion. So, maybe I can work on this some more." I jotted "Lead" on the pink Post-it and placed it at the start of the nomination.

You might choose to simply have children use a pencil to mark up their writing, though the colorful Post-its act as flags to remind children where they have decided to put their attention.

"Did you see how I used the checklist to look back at the parts of my nomination to think about what I am doing well and to make plans for what *else* I can do to make my piece even better? I looked at each part of the checklist to determine if I am doing what second-grade opinion writers are expected to do or if I'm already doing some of the things third-graders are expected to do."

ACTIVE ENGAGEMENT

Give students an opportunity to begin to self-assess their nomination writing using the Opinion Writing Checklist.

"Now it's your turn to try this. First, put the nomination that you decided is your best work in front of you. You'll find some Post-its in your writing folder: green ones (remember, for go!) and pink ones (remember, for stop!). I have copies of the Opinion Writing Checklist for each of you to use, too! You can get started, right here on the rug. I'll come around to listen in and help you out if you need me." As students worked, I circulated among them, supporting those who needed some additional scaffolding.

Coach children to listen not only for what they already do well, but also for what they want to do even better, setting goals for themselves.

After just a few minutes, I called the group back together. "Writers, many of you are finding that you did lots of things already in your writing, and that is great. But to become a much better writer, you also need to be hard on yourself and to be able to say, 'I can do more. I could be *even better* at this. Read your writing very carefully. Work as a revision detective. What are you noticing in your writing? What can you do to make your writing even stronger and more powerful?' I know you'll want to talk to your partner about this important work. Go ahead, tell your partner, which of these could become your own personal goals?" After children talked for a bit, I gave each child an index card and asked them to record a goal or two for themselves.

Listen in to students' self-evaluations, and encourage them to find evidence of their strengths in more than one piece of writing.

"Writers, tell each other what you do well!" I said and listened in for a minute. "Now prove it. Show your partner your Post-its, and give your partner proof!"

I gave them a minute to show off. "Listen, writers, what matters is not that you can do one of these things in one piece of writing. What's important is that you do this all the time as a writer. Can you take one of the things you said you're good at, and can you find evidence that you did this good writing work in other pieces? Once you've found some places, show your partner. Really show off, so you'll know it's not just this one time; it's you as a writer."

The children dove into their nominations, putting fresh Post-its on pages, showing their work proudly to their partners. Reasonably, for some, it was hard to find more evidence of some work in earlier writing from the unit.

Be sure to coach your students as they use the checklist. Often children who check everything off quickly—finding little to improve—are actually having trouble identifying the elements on the checklist in their writing. When you see this happening, you might say, "I see you checked off . . . Where did you do that? Did you do it again and again? Where? If it is hard to find can you find a place where you might try it?"

Crystallize a few goals that many children seem to have identified, doing this in a way that reinforces these goals. Here, we'll shout about them (in whispers).

"Writers, I am so proud of you for setting such determined goals. This is really going to let you be more independent. You just taught yourself to set important writing goals!

"Now, let's whisper-shout about our goals! If you decided to get *even better* at telling a big, strong opinion, whisper-shout 'opinion!' Then look around at writers who set the same goal. Take note, because you'll want to sit near someone who has the same goal today." They whisper-shouted, gleefully.

"Okay, now if you decided to get even better at giving examples, whisper-shout 'examples,' and look around to see who shares your goal.

"If you set a goal of getting better at beginnings, whisper-shout 'beginnings,' and notice your buddies.

"And finally, if one of your goals is getting better at endings, whisper-shout 'endings'! See who you are? Very exciting."

LINK

Channel children to sit near other writers who are working on the same goal so they can help each other and show off their work.

"Now, writers, let's get to work independently, but this time, sit near other writers who share one of your goals. That way, you can help each other, and you can show off your work.

"So for now, quickly decide which goal you'll be working on first today. Is it beginnings? Endings? Strong opinions? Giving examples?"

I'd soon organized writers who wanted to work on one goal toward one area of the classroom, those who wanted to work on another goal to another area, and so on, often putting kids into partnerships to help them focus. "You are going to be writing right next to writers who share your goal, so you can help each other and show off the new strategies you are developing."

Making goals public is a great way to solidify them. It also teaches a valuable lesson—namely, that having goals does not mean we are deficient as writers. Setting goals is something all writers do to outgrow themselves.

Self-grouping by goals is a great way to put your kids into small groups. It makes it easier for you to teach efficiently, and the children can support each other too.

Putting Yourself Out of a Job

NOW THAT YOUR CHILDREN HAVE SELF-ASSESSED and put themselves into groups, you can set them up to teach each other, make their own tools, and generally outgrow you for a while. This will likely be one of those days when you can move around the room like a butterfly, pausing at each of your lovely flowers only briefly to admire them and do some cross-pollination work. Take, for example, my meeting with Petra.

Petra was hard at work on her goal to included examples to support ideas. She wanted the examples to come from her life, from the book, and from other things she knew. I looked down at her paper to see which part she was working on. I didn't want to spend our time having her read to me and thus pull her away from what she was doing. Her writing is shown in Figure 17–1.

Petra wasn't looking at her writing at all. Her nose was in her book and she had Post-its in hand. "Petra, you are so hard at work. What are you doing to work toward your goal?" Of course, the four children sitting near her were working on the same goal, so as I spoke to her I looked for them to listen in.

(continues)

> Stink moody is a nut! His name is stink and he actuly lets people call him that. Also in this book, Stink is all exited to go on a field trip to an exibit about yuky smells. Isn't that gross?

FIG. 17–1   An excerpt from Petra's nomination

Celebrating and Setting New Goals

"Writers, let's have a celebration *before* the celebration. As I look around the room I see two amazing things. First, I see children working together and teaching each other. I see kids pointing to each other's writing, giving great advice about places to grow in writing. Give a thumbs up if you have been working together and teaching your classmates." Every thumb in the room was raised high in the air.

"I saw something else too. The second amazing thing I'm noticing is that writers across this room are actually meeting, and *exceeding*, their goals. You may not have realized it yet, but many of you have been working so hard this whole time, and now your writing really shows that you can even do many of the things third-graders are expected to do! Do you want to prove it?" The class cheered and I continued. "Let's put our goals in one hand and our writing in front of us. Now, reread the goal and slowly page through your writing. You can tap your writing at each of the places where you worked on your goal. Go ahead!" As children did this I moved around the room, giving kids smiles of approval and encouraging them to do the same for their classmates.

After a few minutes, I called for their attention again. "Did you prove it? Did you show that you have already met some of your goals?" The class cheered again. "Congratulations, writers. You can shake each other's hands for an accomplishment like that!

"This is so exciting. Meeting goals can only mean one thing. You know what comes next right? Now we need new goals!" I quickly handed out smaller copies of the checklist and had children put a star next to their new goals, but not until they got a chance to cross off the goals they had already achieved."

"Oh, I'm looking back in my book for more examples of Stink being a nut. I mean on this page," she pointed to the page she was reading, "he is actually walking through a giant nose and saying, 'This is more fun than earwax!' That is totally nuts. I have to add it to my writing!" I was proud of Petra's progress—as was she—but I was even more impressed by her classmates' reactions. As she spoke two of them grabbed their own books. This was my chance to voice over the strategy Petra had taught them and encourage them to keep helping each other.

"Writers, sitting near people who have the same goal is great, because you can teach each other. As Petra started talking about looking in her book for more examples, I saw Levi and Sarah start doing the same! Wow! You must be proud of yourselves!

"Now if you were to make a little reminder chart for your group, what would you call it?"

"Ways to find examples!" Sarah offered. The others nodded, and I quickly started a mini-chart by writing the words on an ordinary piece of white paper.

"Well, now we will need some strategies on this chart. What should we start with?"

"I'll add my strategy: 'look in a book.'" Petra said. I handed her a Post-it so she could write down the strategy and put it on the mini-chart.

"I was thinking of things I just know," Sarah said. "Like, I don't know it from a book. I am writing about *The Twits*. I have a part from the book where he doesn't take baths. I am going to add that if you don't take a bath dirt gets stuck to your body. My mom says that's why you're sick. You know, if you get a cold or something. *And* I know that from science class too." I handed Sarah a Post-it so she could add to the chart as well.

"I'm gonna try that too, maybe in this one or in my *Dork Diaries* nomination." Petra added.

Before leaving the group, I said, "So, writers, you can teach each other all of the ways you can work toward your goals. When you try a new strategy, I know you will want to add it to your group chart so you can all continue to learn from each other."

I moved on to others, offering similar kinds of compliment groups, where I found one child working successfully, helped him to share his methods with his classmates, and then encouraged the group to make a chart and continue supporting each other. Voila! I'm out of a job and the children are officially the teachers!

Sharing Student-Made Tools and Strategies

Ask small groups to share the strategies that they used to help them meet their writing goals.

"Writers, join me on the rug. Let's share all the smart strategies you invented today. Bring your group charts and writing folders." I asked them to sit with their goal groups.

"Writers, you've worked so hard on your goals! What was most impressive was how you worked together, teaching each other strategies to reach those goals. You even discovered ways to take on new work to be successful as writers." I counted the ways across my fingers. "You learned that you can: one, study a checklist. Two, use what you know about writing. Three, learn a strategy from a classmate. Four, make a chart to remember it all!" The class followed along, patting each other on the backs.

"But we're not done! Now that you have chosen new goals, let's share the strategies you've come up with to help your friends meet their goals. When you share, you might decide to use your writing to demonstrate how to use the strategy by showing what *you* did. Which group would like to share first?"

Each group shared their tabletop charts, naming the strategies they tried, while others from the group chimed in to explain exactly how some of the strategies worked, even offering examples from their own writing. Zac showed the class how he drew a picture of a part in his book and then labeled both the characters and their actions to make his ideas clearer. The children also noticed that strategies like "look in the book" helped for many different goals—a very important realization about transfer and application.

"Do you see a strategy or two from one of the groups' charts that could help you to meet your newest goals?" When they thought that yes, in fact, they had, I invited them to jot down the strategy (or strategies) they planned to use, sticking a Post-it note on their folder to remind them to do this work during the final days of the unit.

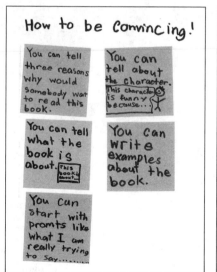

FIG. 17–2

Keeping the Elaboration Going

ear Teachers,

You are in the home stretch, with the final celebration in sight! Today your students will have lots to focus their attention on. In fact, you may find that your students can live off the teaching you did in the last session for days! The purpose of this letter is to suggest that for the remainder of this bend—whether one day or three—you let the work your students have done to develop strategy charts guide their final revisions. You may decide to gather your students together to remind them to call upon their partners, reference their checklists and charts, and make their own plan for their writing. If you set out high and lofty ambitions without providing children time to carry out those ambitions, they are bound to become frustrated or come to believe that they will not be held accountable to this higher standard of work. This can even lead to growing hesitation when faced with lofty ambitions in the future. So here, we will suggest a plan for helping your students to continue helping themselves.

MINILESSON

You might begin this lesson by inviting your students to look over the goals and strategies they planned during yesterday's share session. The work they did was ambitious, and now you will want to support them as they put those plans into action. We suggest your focus for today's lesson be more about study skills than writing skills, because after all, they are forever intertwined. You might talk to your students about how to keep themselves going. You could say, "Today I want to teach you that writers work hard toward their goals, and when they meet those goals, they reexamine their writing and set brand-new goals." It is a continual process: work toward goals, try new strategies, meet goals, set new ones! You might use this teaching as an opportunity to introduce a process chart illustrating this ongoing cycle of work.

As you move into the demonstration, show children how you use the checklist to recall the goals you set yesterday, then retell the strategy you will use to work toward that goal. As you retell the strategy, you'll want to reference the mini-chart that houses the strategy described. You might say, "Now how did that strategy work again? Oh yes, it is on the chart that Sarah shared yesterday! Yes, there it is. Now I remember. She said that one way to add to my opinion is to tell some information that I know from my life, just like she added that Mr. Twit should take a bath, because she learned in science that dirt can make you sick! Okay, so I can add information I know, hmm, let me try finding a spot where I can do that." As you demonstrate this process, remember to bring the children all the way through the cycle, modeling the way one goal leads to the next and the next. Be mindful of pace during today's demonstration. Children do not need to watch you go through every tiny detail of the process—reaching for every word, pondering what goal to choose, and so on. The important part is that they observe how you follow through with your planned work and move on to choose new work.

During the active engagement, you may choose to ask children to coach each other in partnerships. You might have Partner 1 name her goal, retell the strategy she will try, mark the exact place where she will try it, then plan ahead for the next goal. As Partner 1 moves through this work, Partner 2 can act as the coach, prompting her to move through the process efficiently. Then, partners can switch roles. This partner work serves three important purposes. First, it gives children time to rehearse the work they will do. Second, the coaching child helps solidify an understanding of the process by articulating the steps. And third, it reinforces children's understanding that they can be each other's teachers.

As you send kids off to write today, you'll want to remind them that this is process work. When you are done, you start again. Make sure they know where all the resources are located in the classroom so that their writing time is active. You might send them off by saying, "Use everything you can to meet your goals. Use checklists. Use class charts. Use our new mini-charts. Use the Wall of Fame. Use one another!"

CONFERRING AND SMALL-GROUP WORK

As your students work toward independence, it will be a great gift for you to help them learn about themselves as writers. We once heard a wise teacher say to a child, "Know yourself as a learner and you can learn anything!" This is quite true. Some writers need space to write. They need to lay all of their papers out so they can see and touch everything. For writers like this, the visual of the pages can help them find new ideas, comb craft throughout their writing, and generally work faster. For other writers, everything must be neat—no paper out of place, otherwise distractions will abound. Some writers really need quiet to concentrate and get their ideas down, while others need to find little stop points along the way, when they can reread, take a stretch, or get some feedback. Without those breaks progress just doesn't occur. It is very important as teachers that we accept that different writers need different things. One of the true challenges of teaching young children is that it is often our job to watch children, notice their patterns for them, and then name them. Thankfully, this will be a great time to do some of that observation work, since the children will be teaching themselves. When you think you have noticed a pattern that might help a child know himself as a learner—and therefore work smarter—discuss it with the child openly. For example you might say, "Levi, I've been watching you, and it seems like you are the kind of learner who writes most when you are in your own head. Sometimes I notice that you tap your head when you are thinking, almost like you are trying to hear your own thoughts. Can you tell me about that?" After a conversation about this, you might help the student find the learning environment he needs. The trick here is to make a celebration out of getting to know yourself as a learner. Don't try to hide the work kids do to make themselves productive. Share it.

MID-WORKSHOP TEACHING

You might find that your children could use a little mid-workshop fun today. The work they are doing is heady, and a little mental stretch could do everyone some good. One teacher I know sometimes stops her students for "shout-outs." In her classroom, shout-outs are a time for children to celebrate each other's accomplishments. This is how it goes. Everyone turns and talks to a partner or classmate, sharing anything they are working on or doing well. Next the teacher says, "Who has a shout-out?" and children respond with comments like, "I have a shout-out for Bea. She wanted to add more examples and supports to her 'Ivy Makes Bean Nicer' chapter, and now she has four examples and a few other things from the book." Then all the children get to hoot and holler for a minute, before the next shout-out. After three or four shout-outs, the kids get back to work, charged up to continue in their pursuits or to take on the strategies of a classmate.

SHARE

Remember that there were two main purposes for today's lesson. One was to give children time to work hard toward big ambitions, and the other was to help children get to know the processes and habits that go along with working hard. Perhaps for today's share you'll ask children to talk about what they have come to learn about themselves as writers. You might ask the class to join you in a circle on the rug and lead by example, starting the share off with something *you* have learned about *yourself* as a writer. I have sometimes shared with kids, "I am the kind of writer who loves to write in peace and quiet. I can write for hours that way. *But* the minute someone talks to me, my ideas get jumbled and I can't think. I need to find a place all by myself to do my best work." Notice how my example stated my learning needs in a positive way and concluded with a strategy I use to do my best work. As children share what they know about their learning, other children can agree with a simple gesture, such as a snap or a thumbs-up signal. While all the children may not be able to share immediately, children will likely make self-discoveries from listening to peers and learn strategies to match those discoveries. This reflective practice can help continue to foster a classroom of thoughtful learners.

Enjoy!

Shanna, Ali, and Liz

Awarding Our Favorites
A Book Fair Celebration

ear Teachers,

Congratulations to you and your writers! Today is a day for celebration—not only for the work your students have produced across this unit, but also for the work you have done to support each child in your classroom. This support serves to foster a community of writers, and readers, who think carefully about books, setting goals for themselves and working thoughtfully to reach those goals. Across this unit, you have encouraged your second-graders to craft letters and nominations that communicate their opinions in structured and compelling ways. And now, what better way to honor these efforts than with a publishing celebration that gives children a forum to recommend their most-loved books, sharing their published nominations aloud with visitors and convincing others to sign up to be the next to read this award winner!

It need not be an extravagant celebration, or even take place outside of your classroom, although imagine how exciting it would be for your students to host their final celebration in the school library or gymnasium, or perhaps even alongside peers from other second-grade classrooms to heighten the celebratory feel! We suggest you invite people outside of your immediate classroom community, perhaps family members or other teachers and classes from the school.

BEFORE THE CELEBRATION

Your students have been working diligently to reflect on their writing, with the aid of a checklist, to revise and edit their pieces to ready them for publication. We suggest that you set up small tables around the classroom, or wherever you decide to host the celebration, with students stationed at each, ready to share their nominations with visitors and talk about these cherished titles to intrigue readers. You may ask each child to display a hard copy of the book at their table or substitute physical copies with printed images of the book or perhaps even student-designed book jackets to capture the eyes of passersby.

Further, the award emblems your children designed in Session 15 might be used now to adhere to their published writing or to a cover page to capture the attention of precisely the kind of reader their book calls for. Don't forget to have sign-up sheets at each station as children share their pieces and convince visitors to sign up on a waiting list and be the next to read it. You may allow visitors to roam freely through the book fair, encouraging them to stop at several displays to learn more about these wonderful books! However, you may decide to structure the celebration in a more systematic fashion—assigning visitors to small groups and asking each group to rotate from display to display.

THE CELEBRATION

As guests arrive, invite them to take a stroll through the fair. Once most of your invited guests are in attendance, you'll likely gather the group's attention to welcome them to the Annual Book Fair of Award Winners and thank everyone for coming. Then, you'll take a brief moment to explain how the celebration will unfold. Tell your guests that they'll tour the book fair with a small group, moving across each display, listening to students' nominations, and signing up on the waiting list to read some of these recommended titles.

Remind your students to speak clearly and with discernible passion, captivating the attention of curious readers. Your students will read from their published writing, but you may prompt children to also speak freely about their opinions, discussing the reasons they feel so strongly about these books, and answering questions guests may have. You may choose to record these book announcements using any accessible audio or visual technology, or to share students' work on a school website or classroom blog! Additionally, you might coordinate with the principal or school librarian to set up a display in the library or main hallway of students' nominations and accompanying books or book jackets to recommend these great reads to the larger school community.

Happy writing! Happy reading! Happy writing about reading!

Ali, Shanna, and Liz

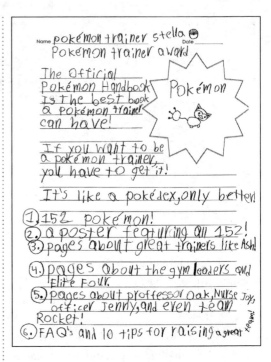

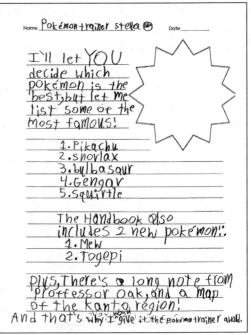

FIG. 19–1   Stella's published piece

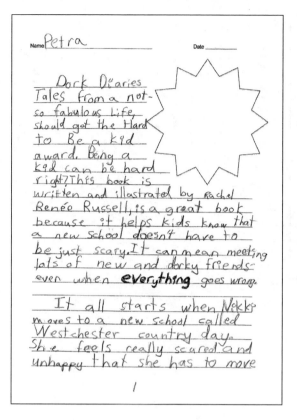

Page 1

Name Petra   Date _____

Dork Diaries Tales from a not-so fabulous Life, should get the Hard to Be a kid award. Being a kid can be hard right? This book is written and illustrated by Rachel Renée Russell, is a great book because it helps kids know that a new school doesn't have to be just scary. It can mean meeting lots of new and dorky friends-even when **everything** goes wrong.

It all starts when Nikki moves to a new school called Westchester country day. She feels really scared and unhappy that she has to move

1

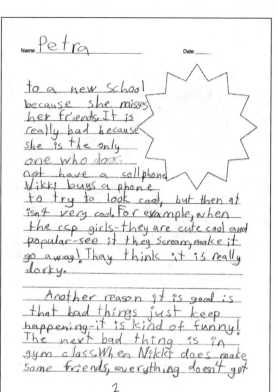

Page 2

Name Petra   Date _____

to a new school because she misses her friends. It is really bad because she is the only one who does not have a cellphone. Nikki buys a phone to try to look cool, but then it isn't very cool. For example, when the ccp girls-they are cute cool and popular-see it they scream, make it go away! They think it is really dorky.

Another reason it is good is that bad things just keep happening-it is kind of funny! The next bad thing is in gym class. When Nikki does make some friends, everything doesn't get

2

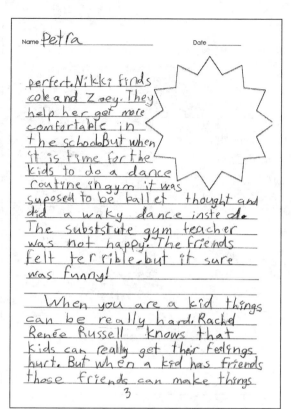

Page 3

Name Petra   Date _____

perfect. Nikki finds cole and Zoey. They help her get more comfortable in the school. But when it is time for the kids to do a dance routine in gym it was suposed to be ballet thought and did a waky dance insted. The substitute gym teacher was not happy. The friends felt terrible. but it sure was funny!

When you are a kid things can be really hard. Rachel Renée Russell knows that kids can really get their feelings hurt. But when a kid has friends those friends can make things

3

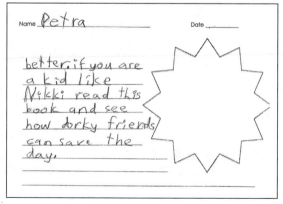

Page 4

Name Petra   Date _____

better. if you are a kid like Nikki read this book and see how dorky friends can save the day.

FIG. 19-2   Petra's published piece

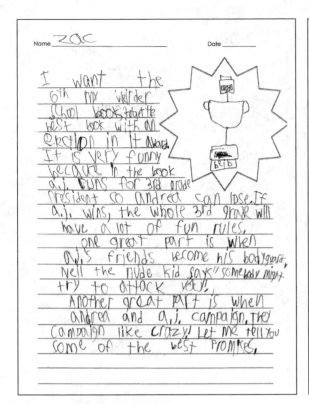

Name ZAC   Date _____

I want the 6th Mr weirder school books, that the best book with an election in it. Award. It is very funny because in the book a.j. runs for 3rd grade president so andrea can lose. If a.j. wins, the whole 3rd grade will have a lot of fun rules.
One great part is when a.j.'s friends become his bodyguard, Neil the nude kid says "somebody might try to attack you".
Another great part is when andrea and a.j. campaign. They campaign like crazy! Let me tell you some of the best promises.

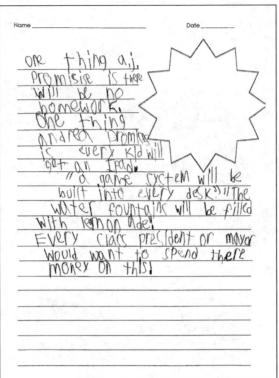

Name _____   Date _____

One thing a.j. promisie is there will be no homework. One thing Andrea promise is every kid will got an iPad. "a game system will be built into every desk." "The water fountains will be filled with lemon ade." Every class president or mayor would want to spend there money on this!

FIG. 19–3 Zac's published piece